PUB WA

── IN ──

Shropshire

Peter Kerr

COUNTRYSIDE BOOKS
NEWBURY, BERKSHIRE

COUNTRYSIDE BOOKS
3 Catherine Road
Newbury, Berkshire

To view our complete range of books,
please visit us at
www.countrysidebooks.co.uk

ISBN 1 85306 668 0

Designed by Graham Whiteman
Maps and photographs by the author
Cover illustration by Colin Doggett

Produced through MRM Associates Ltd., Reading
Printed by J. W. Arrowsmith Ltd., Bristol

Contents

AREA MAP SHOWING THE LOCATION OF THE WALKS

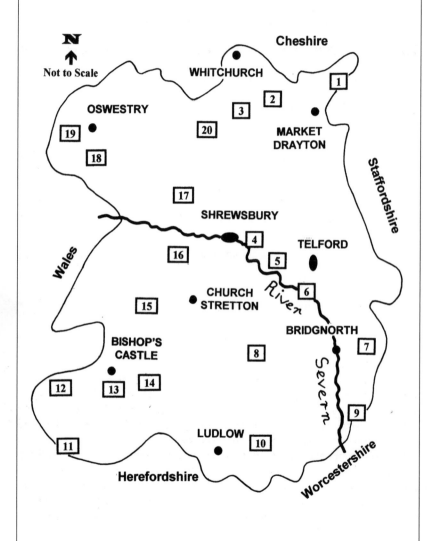

Walk

Publisher's Note

We hope that you obtain considerable enjoyment from this book; great care has been taken in its preparation. However, changes of landlord and actual closures are sadly not uncommon. Likewise, although at the time of publication all routes followed public rights of way or permitted paths, diversion orders can be made and permissions withdrawn.

We cannot, of course, be held responsible for such diversion orders and any inaccuracies in the text which result from these or any other changes to the routes nor any damage which might result from walkers trespassing on private property. We are anxious though that all details covering the walks and the pubs are kept up to date and would therefore welcome information from readers that would be relevant to future editions.

The sketch maps accompanying each walk are not always to scale and are intended to guide you to the starting point and give a simple but accurate idea of the route to be taken. For those who like the benefit of detailed maps, we recommend that you arm yourself with the relevant Ordnance Survey map in the Explorer series.

INTRODUCTION

The research and writing of this new *Pub Walks* book for Shropshire provided an interesting and thoroughly enjoyable challenge – the 20 excellent pubs included in this collection were finally selected from over 50 visited, the choice being based on the quality of the food and drink, the location for an interesting and enjoyable walk, and that the pub was open most weekday lunchtimes with the possible exception of the winter months.

As the pub and the walk are both part of the outing, the rambles have been kept to a reasonable half day's excursion. Another factor considered was how to provide walks that reflect the differing geography of the county and thus have a mixture of hilly and flatter routes; this was soon resolved by locating the walks as evenly as possible throughout the county, five in each quadrant. If an imaginary line is drawn diagonally across Shropshire, from Oswestry in the north-west, through Shrewsbury, to Bridgnorth in the south-east, then north of that line the county is flatter, to the south, generally hilly. The walk numbers therefore start at the top and go clockwise around the county; this gives a good mixture of varied terrain and the prominent high points (The Wrekin, for example) can be viewed from differing angles.

Several of the routes pass places of great historic interest and, when these are open to the public as attractions, I recommend you consider a separate visit either before or after your walk. They include Wroxeter Roman town, the Coalport Museum near Ironbridge, Stokesay Castle at Craven Arms, and All Saints Church in Claverley.

Another aim of the book has been to ensure that interesting, but less frequently visited, locations have been used for the walks such as Norton in Hales, Calverhall, Platt Lane, Llanfair Waterdine, Lydbury North, Myddle, Candy and Loppington, places which a number of people I spoke to did not know existed. A deliberate inclusion has been some small sections of the five 'long distance' routes that are within, or pass through, the county. These are the Shropshire Way (Walks 3, 5, 10 and 15), the Jack Mytton Way (Walk 11), the Offa's Dyke Path (Walks 11, 12 and 19), the Marches Way (Walk 17) and the Severn Way (Walks 4 and 6).

The variety of paths used was similarly considered so as to include country lanes, old green lanes, bridleways and footpaths, all the routes being on rights of way with some minor exceptions where 'permissive paths' have been used. (These permissive paths are the canal towpath in Walk 3, and some nature reserve paths, Walks 16 and 18.) All the path included were open and usable when the walks were researched but, with time, problems can occur. If a path problem is encountered it would help future ramblers if these could be reported to Shropshire County Council, Countryside Service Section, Shirehall, Abbey Foregate, Shrewsbury SY2 6ND (telephone: 01743 255055), so that they can be resolved.

There is usually a car park for customers at the pub – in each case the starting (and finishing) point of the walk. If you are not visiting the pub, please choose your parking spot carefully nearby and be sure that you are not blocking any exits/entrances or farm gates.

In closing I hope that the reader will have as much enjoyment as my wife, Olive, and I did in seeking out this selection of walks and seeing a number of places we had not previously visited. My wife was also very helpful in giving the final verdict on whether a route was enjoyable enough to include. If you already know Shropshire perhaps this book can introduce you to new places for walking; if you are new to the area I hope it will show you what a wealth of history and variety of scenery there is throughout this beautiful county.

Peter Kerr

NORTON IN HALES, NEAR MARKET DRAYTON: THE HINDS HEAD

This is a beautiful walk that starts from a picturesque village on the Shropshire/Staffordshire border and uses a mixture of field paths, bridleways, old green lanes, and quiet country roads. A gentle, easy ramble which allows you to forget the hustle and bustle of everyday life and enjoy sweeping views towards Staffordshire and Cheshire.

The village of Norton in Hales is only just in Shropshire, the village centre being no more than 500 yards from the River Tern, the county boundary with Staffordshire. As it is away from any main road it retains a rural and quiet atmosphere with two of the main focal points of the village being within sight of each other, the pub and the church. Between the two, on the small village green, is the 'Bradling' or 'Bumping' stone, reputed to be the site for punishing people still working after noon on a Shrove Tuesday. The pub, the Hinds Head, dating from the early 18th century and recorded as being a 'pick up'

point for stagecoaches between Market Drayton and Staffordshire, has been considerably extended and tastefully modernised. It now boasts a large lounge area with open fireplace (the original part of the building), a dining area with an old post-box, exposed beams, and a public bar with a large TV screen. All in all a relaxing and comfortable village pub.

As may be expected from an establishment that cannot rely on passing trade but needs to actively attract customers from a wide area, the choice of food is extensive, from a large range of bar snacks to a full restaurant menu. Bar snacks include their special toasted Hinds Head club sandwiches, baguettes, salads, jacket potatoes and a selection of sandwiches with unusual fillings, (such as honey, pecan and banana). The full menu includes such dishes as Brie Wedges, Lamb Shrewsbury and steaks from the charcoal grill. There are also daily specials and my choice of a smoked salmon and prawn salad was ideal for a warm sunny day. The beer range includes Courage Director's, Boddingtons Bitter, Theakston Best Bitter and John Smith's Extra Smooth. The lagers are Stella Artois, Kronenbourg 1664 and Carlsberg and there is also Strongbow cider and Guinness. Add to this a wine list and a display cabinet full of tempting puddings and it is possible that a post-lunch walk may not even be started! Meals are available on Monday to Saturday from 12 noon to 2.30 pm and 6.30 pm to 9.30 pm and on Sunday from 12 noon to 6 pm.

Telephone: 01630 653014.

- **HOW TO GET THERE:** Norton in Hales is located 3 miles north-east of Market Drayton; it is signposted from the A53 and the B5415.
- **PARKING:** There is a large car park for customers at the side of the pub – please advise staff if leaving your car while you walk.
- **LENGTH OF THE WALK:** 5½ miles. Map: OS Explorer 243 Market Drayton (GR 703386).

THE WALK

1. Leaving the front entrance of the pub turn left, follow the lane past Griffin Close, then turn left immediately past the next house. Proceed through a field, left edge, negotiating two kissing gates, enter a lane and turn right. Now enjoy the gentle walk along the lane, generally with pasture land to the left and arable fields to the right. Go around some bends (the imposing dwelling to the left is Brand Hall) then, just past the buttresses of an old railway bridge, enter the field by going through two gates set at right angles to each other.

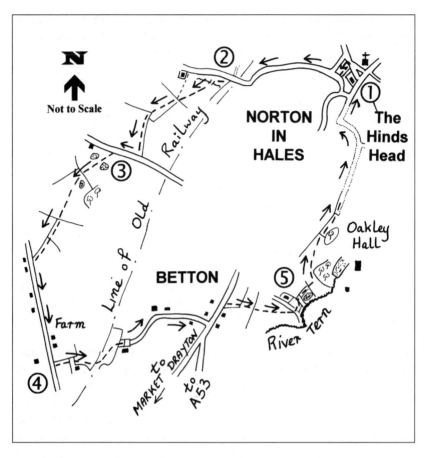

2. Once in the field go diagonally across it, initially almost parallel to the electricity poles. Cross a culvert bridge, then converge with the electricity poles to pass under the cables to a stile and gate by a lone tree. Cross the next field parallel to the hedge on the left, use another gate or stile and then follow the left hedge. At the road turn right then, after about 300 yards, cross a stile on the left.

3. From the stile go part right passing between two small ponds surrounded by bushes; directly ahead the view is over North Shropshire and to the right is Cheshire. Proceed to a gate in the hedge and then go part left, pass another small pond on the left, then continue over the large open field aiming just to the left of the timber-framed house visible ahead. Cross a stile by a tree then follow the right hedge, over two more stiles, to reach a lane. Turn left and follow the lane for just over ½ mile, to a point some 200 yards past Bettonmoss Farm; here take the stile on the left. On the lane the view left is towards Staffordshire.

4. Now cross a field, use a gate then another stile, then go part right to reach the tree line. Soon cross a small corner of a field and then go over the disused rail line, the same one passed near point 2. Go diagonally across the next field aiming to the left of the house on the opposite side. Cross a stile and pass the house, going over more stiles, to reach a lane, and follow it as it bends right to reach a road junction at Betton. The now disused corrugated iron church was built in1886 and was used up to the 1980s; it is of a type produced for use as missionary churches in the British Colonies. At the road junction go left and, after passing the last house on the right, go through a kissing gate on the right. Follow the right fence, then cross a small field, and continue in the same general direction over the next large field, aiming to the right of the house ahead. Eventually reach a stile to a gravel track on the far side of the field.

5. Cross a stile to a garden, after the next stile go part left up the bank, then join an enclosed path, pond on the right. The stream over to the right is the River Tern, the boundary between Shropshire and Staffordshire. Soon cross a footbridge and stile and go over the field to a wall and turn left. The large building ahead/right is Oakley Hall. Initially follow the wall and, as it turns right, only go part right aiming for a large tree to the right of a small hill. Continue to the far left corner of the field, go through a gate, then follow the left fence and low wall. Go through a bridlegate and follow an old green lane which soon joins a gravel track, then follow the track back to Norton in Hales.

CALVERHALL, NEAR WHITCHURCH
THE OLD JACK INN

Plenty of variety here in a walk through the North Shropshire countryside, initially using field paths, to visit the village of Ightfield and the hamlet of Ash Parva. The route then follows bridlepaths, green lanes and quiet country roads to return to Calverhall, giving the opportunity to 'step out' whilst admiring the sweeping views towards Wales.

Calverhall (or Corra), a much younger village than neighbouring Ightfield, was reputed to be the home of a drinking vessel, made of leather and lined with horn, called the 'Jack of Corra'. It was a challenge to drink all the contents in one go (this due to its design) and it was kept at the local pub, now the Old Jack Inn. The vessel disappeared in 1860 (perhaps someone took it home to finish the beer) but the inn remains and is the base for this walk. Built in 1811 as an ale house, it is now a warm, friendly pub with award-winning food. The attractive beamed bar area invites relaxation, the bar itself is

12

adorned with carved wood panelling, there is an interesting display of miniature drinks bottles and, at the rear, a large restaurant.

As might be expected from an award-winning pub the bar menu includes sandwiches, salads, grills, fish, a savoury selection and vegetarian dishes. There are also daily specials such as Lamb Henry (my choice, a large lamb shank in rich gravy), rib steak and a selection of fish dishes. In the evening there is also a full à la carte menu in the restaurant. The beers available include Worthington Creamflow, Caffrey's Irish Ale, Guinness and guest beers (changed regularly), such as Hancock's HB Bitter and Robinson's Best Bitter. The lagers are Beck's and Carling and the cider is Dry Blackthorn. There is also a good selection of bottles of wine from around the world. Food is usually available from 12 noon to 2 pm on Tuesday to Saturday, (2.15 pm on Sunday). In the evening the times are 6.30 pm to 9.30 pm on Monday to Friday (10 pm on Saturday and 9 pm on Sunday).

Telephone: 01948 890235.

- **HOW TO GET THERE:** Calverhall is situated between Whitchurch and Market Drayton on an unclassified road linking it with Ightfield and Bletchley. It is signposted from the A41.
- **PARKING:** Customers can use the pub car park – please advise the owners if leaving your car while you walk.
- **LENGTH OF THE WALK:** 6½ miles. Maps: OS Explorer 241 Shrewsbury and 243 Market Drayton (GR 602373).

THE WALK

1. On leaving the pub turn right and follow the lane (signposted to Market Drayton) past a farm and houses then, some 100 yards past the last house on the left, turn left onto a track (part tarmac). At the end cross a stile then follow the right hedge, go through the gate ahead and continue part left across a large field, keeping to the right of a small group of trees. At the far hedge go over two stiles and a ditch crossing (care needed, deep ditch) then aim for the left of the group of trees (surrounding a pond) at the far end of the field. Cross the stile beyond the pond and go slightly left, aiming for the houses in the distance, and on approaching them use the stile and track on the left to reach the road.

2. Turn right at the road to reach the village of Ightfield, an old settlement that was mentioned in the Domesday Book. At the next

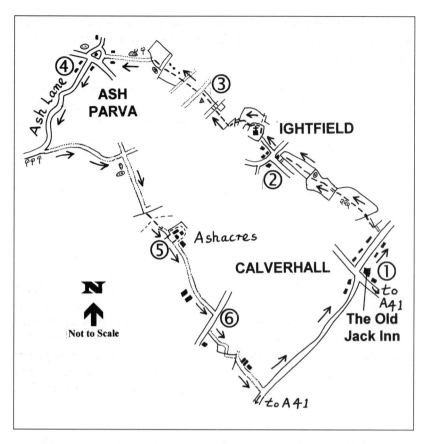

junction turn right (signposted to Burleydam) and after 50 yards take the lane on the left to reach the church, dedicated to St John the Baptist. It is worth looking at some of the exterior carvings, the gargoyles and the ornate churchyard cross. On entering the churchyard the route is immediately right along the hedge, ignore the gate at the first corner and generally follow the hedge to reach a stile just past the next corner (beyond the headstone of one, George Arkinstall). Now follow the left tree/hedge line, then cross the field to a stile and ditch crossing (care needed again, deep ditch that may be hidden by undergrowth). Follow the right hedge to a gate and go through, now go slightly left, aiming well to the left of a mound (a reservoir). Cross more stiles with a ditch crossing between (deep, water-filled ditch) then follow the right hedge, past an old OS triangulation column, to reach a tarmac drive. This path gives sweeping views of the surrounding countryside; to the left the Breiddens are prominent, also the high border area beyond Oswestry, to the right the view is towards Cheshire and Staffordshire.

3. At the tarmac drive turn left for about 50 yards, cross a stile on the right, then go directly across the field. Cross a grassy track and proceed over the next field, generally following (on the right) a line of electricity poles. At the far side of the field cross two stiles, follow the left fence/hedge then, about 100 yards from the end of the field, look for a stile and gate on the left (may be partially hidden). Now follow an old green lane to reach the hamlet of Ash Parva. At a fork keep right, joining a tarmac lane, then at the next junction turn left to reach the village pond.

4. This latter part of the walk gives the opportunity to stride out along quiet country roads and wide tracks. Cross the road and take the narrow lane opposite the pond, Ash Lane. Follow this as it meanders for over ½ mile, with views towards Wales, to reach a point where it turns right with a small wood to the left of the lane. Here turn sharp left, joining a wide track, which is now followed and has a sweeping view, right, towards the Breiddens. Just after the track sweeps left reach a track junction and turn right, onto another wide track, with ponds on the right. On reaching a gate go through, cross the field, then join another track to reach a farm, Ashacres.

5. The route is now directly through the farmyard to join the drive at the other side (there is a side gate by the solid-looking gate ahead). However, if the yard is full of cattle, there is a permissive route around the left side of the farm, simply use the gate on the left, just prior to the first barn, then follow the signs around the back of the buildings to reach the drive at the front of the house. Continue down the drive, passing more farm buildings on the right, to reach a road.

6. Now turn right, follow the road for 200 yards then, just prior to another farm, go through a gate on the left. First follow the right hedge then keep on the track as it goes into the field and turns right. Go through a gate, turn left, follow the hedge to another gate and turn right. Now follow the track straight through the farmyard, past the farmhouse, and follow the drive to the road. Here turn left and continue on the lane for one mile back to Calverhall.

PLATT LANE, WHIXALL, NEAR WHITCHURCH: THE WAGGONERS INN

This walk begins at a delightful pub beside the Llangollen Canal. The route visits the former peat cutting area of Fenn's Moss, joins a section of the canal, then returns via some attractive field paths and part of the Shropshire Way long distance path. You will enjoy some sweeping views towards the Welsh hills.

The parish of Whixall, on the Welsh/English border, covers an extensive area of farming country with scattered farms and small hamlets such as Hollinwood and Welsh End. Within this maze of narrow country lanes, at a road junction known as Platt Lane, is the Waggoners Inn, a small country pub that is the social hub of the community and a pleasant refuge for travellers by road or canal. Thought to have been built in the early 1800s, as a farmhouse, it subsequently developed into one of the two ale houses by the Platt

16

Lane junction (the other one is now a private house). It then became the regular meeting place of the peat cutters who worked the 'Moss' and as such, passing strangers were not welcomed. Today, however, very little peat is cut and the canal brings 'strangers' from all over the world, particularly in the summer months, to this now welcoming pub with its cosy bar, games room, separate restaurant and large garden with tables.

The pub's main trade comes from the local community and boating enthusiasts using the canal, so the banter can cover issues from around the world, depending on the nationality of the boaters on that particular day. The food available also reflects the wishes of the same customers, straightforward, well-prepared dishes using as many local ingredients as possible – for example, beef (fillet, sirloin, rump or rib, served plain or with a rich sauce) through to mixed grills, duck and chicken. For people wanting something more exotic there is a range of balti meals and a choice of starters and puddings. On my lunchtime visit, a Sunday, I enjoyed the 'Special of the Day', local roast rib of beef, and this in a pub full of local families all enjoying the food, a sure sign of a good eating place. The beers available are Bass, Worthington Bitter, Caffrey's Irish Ale and M&B Mild. There is also Blackthorn cider, Carling lager, Guinness and house wine for those who don't drink beer. Food times, from March to October are 12 noon to 10 pm, all week. From November to February food is available as above at weekends but only from 4.30 pm on weekdays, the winter opening time for the pub.
Telephone: 01948 880259.

- **HOW TO GET THERE:** A test of navigational skills. First locate Tilstock on the B5476, some 3 miles south of Whitchurch, then take the lane going west (Maltkiln Lane on the OS map), signposted to Whixall, and go through Hollinwood to reach the pub at the Platt Lane junction.
- **PARKING:** Customers can use the pub car park but please ask first. In the winter, when the pub is closed weekday lunchtimes, there are spaces at the side of the road opposite the car park entrance.
- **LENGTH OF THE WALK:** 5½ miles. Map: OS Explorer 241 Shrewsbury (GR 514364).

The Walk

1. From the front entrance of the pub turn right down the road and cross over the Llangollen Canal. As the road sweeps right continue ahead on a narrower lane, and on reaching houses turn right. Follow

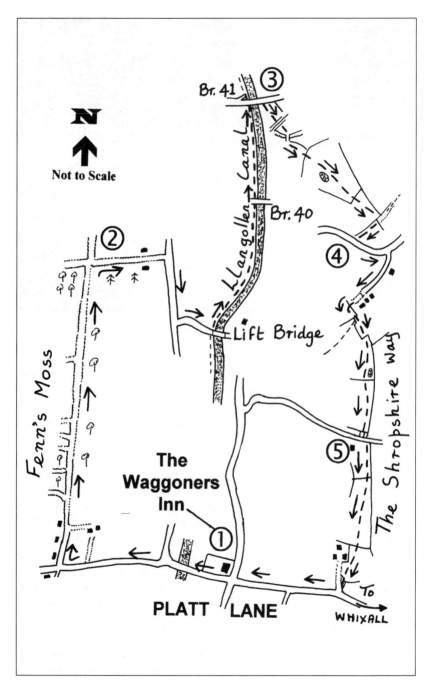

Dutch-style lift bridge on the Llangollen Canal.

this tarmac lane (have your passport ready) and continue straight ahead when it becomes a stony track (you are now in Wales). The route is now along the eastern edge of Fenn's Moss which together with the adjacent Whixall, Bettisfield and Cadney Mosses form the third largest raised bog in Britain – a notice board on the route gives more details. Continue along the wide track with glimpses, left, of the hills beyond Oswestry. The track is a right of way but, as Fenn's Moss is of considerable importance for its wildlife and plants, people are requested not to enter it without a permit. At one time the Moss was extensively worked for peat but this work has all but ceased with the area becoming a nature reserve. The bogginess of the ground did cause considerable problems when the Llangollen Canal (then called the Ellesmere Canal) was constructed in the late 1790s, making this section one of the most difficult to build. Soon more open views across the Moss, left, are encountered, then the track again enters woodland and reaches a path crossroads, where you turn right.

2. Continue along this, also wide, track away from the Moss, past farm buildings, and turn right at a road. Follow the road, turn left at the next junction, then at the canal turn left onto the towpath (now safely back in England). The Dutch-style lift bridge here (this steel one having replaced the earlier wooden one) is a feature of parts of the Llangollen Canal, these being cheaper than stone bridges. Now walk along the canal, passing under a stone bridge (No 40 – notice the grooves worn by towropes). At the second bridge (No 41), go under, turn left to reach a lane, cross over the canal and take a stile on the right.

3. Once in the field go very slightly left to reach, at the far tree line, two stiles with a muddy ditch between (jump!). Now aim slightly right, across the field corner, to a footbridge and once over turn left. Follow the left field edge around the first corner and after about 50 yards cross a stile by a tree. Proceed directly across the large field, keep right of a hollow (possibly with water) to reach a stile near the centre of the far hedge. Here the views to the rear are across Wales to the hills beyond Oswestry and Wrexham. In the next field go to the far left corner, cross a stile and turn right, joining the Shropshire Way, identified by the buzzard symbol, the head acting as a directional arrow. This part of the Shropshire Way is known as the Northern Extension, joining the main circuit, at Wem, to Grindley Brook by the Cheshire border, thus giving a link to Cheshire's Sandstone Trail. Now follow the right hedge over two more stiles to reach a road and turn left.

4. Follow the road for about 300 yards to turn right up a lane, just past a left bend in the road. Continue ahead past farm buildings and farmhouse on the left (this new path differs from the OS map) to reach the end of an enclosed track. Directly ahead the three hills visible are the Breiddens. Enter the field and turn left, cross a stile at the next field corner and then continue ahead, ignoring the stile in the right fence. Follow the right fence to another stile and then follow the left fence/hedge, through two fields to a lane, accessed by gate or stile. If using the stile, care is needed, there is a deep ditch with ditch crossing on the lane side.

5. Cross the lane, go through a bridlegate, then follow the left hedge to a gate into the next field. Now go slightly right, aiming for the left side of the farm buildings ahead to reach another bridlegate. Go through and continue ahead to reach the far right corner of the field. Go through yet another bridlegate to join a drive, follow that to a road then turn right to return to the pub.

UCKINGTON, NEAR SHREWSBURY
THE HORSESHOE INN
❦

This is a walk with plenty of scenic delights, and historical ones too. There is a visit to the important Roman town of Wroxeter, and a working 'Roman' vineyard. You will travel a short section of the Severn Way and there are dramatic views across the Severn Valley to Caer Caradoc.

The present size of the Horseshoe Inn belies its past history as a coaching inn on the old A5, London to Holyhead, road. Believed to have its origins in the 18th century, it became part of the Brewers Fayre chain in the early 1990s. They extended and tastefully decorated the premises to provide a large bar and spacious dining areas, some being non-smoking, the present bar being in the original building. The inn now has two large car parks, a garden, children's play areas inside and outside, and a dining conservatory with a superb view of The Wrekin.

As might be expected of a large company the range of food and drink is wide. The beers on offer include Boddingtons, Wadworth 6X and regular guests such as Old Speckled Hen and Shropshire Lad. The lagers available are Heineken and Stella Artois, the cider is Strongbow and, as always, there is Guinness. For wine drinkers there is a list of wines from around the world. The food is equally impressive, there being a full range of starters, main courses, puddings, lighter snacks, a good vegetarian selection and a special menu for children. In addition there is always a selection of daily specials which on my visit included Dijon Chicken, Salmon Balmoral and Pepperpot Pork. My choice on the day was from the main menu, their Chicken and Steak Platter, this being a rump steak, cooked to perfection, accompanied by a double chicken breast. A big 'plus' for this pub are the times of food availability, meals being served seven days a week from 11.30 am to 10 pm.

Telephone: 01952 740238.

- **HOW TO GET THERE:** The Horseshoe Inn is located on the B5061, some 5 miles east of Shrewsbury.
- **PARKING:** There are two large car parks for customers – please advise the manager if leaving your car while you walk.
- **LENGTH OF THE WALK**: 5½ miles. Map: OS Explorer 241 Shrewsbury (GR 577094).

THE WALK

1. From the front of the inn turn left and follow the narrow lane, which is on the line of the old Roman road, Watling Street, leading to Viroconium. Soon the Breidden Hills come into view ahead/right then, extending southwards, there are Long Mountain and The Long Mynd, finishing with Caer Caradoc and The Lawley ahead/left. At a road junction turn left then cross the B4380 to reach the ruins of the Roman town of Viroconium. At its height this town was the fourth largest town in Roman Britain and the ruins visible today are but a small part of the overall town area. Indeed, its perimeter defences extended beyond the present village of Wroxeter. The site is administered by English Heritage and is open to the public. Further details are available from the site office, telephone: 01743 761330. A separate visit here is recommended; or perhaps after your walk?

2. Continue past the Roman ruins, The Wrekin dramatically positioned behind the remaining high wall of the Basilica. Soon the Severn Way is joined and the walk continues through the village of Wroxeter with the

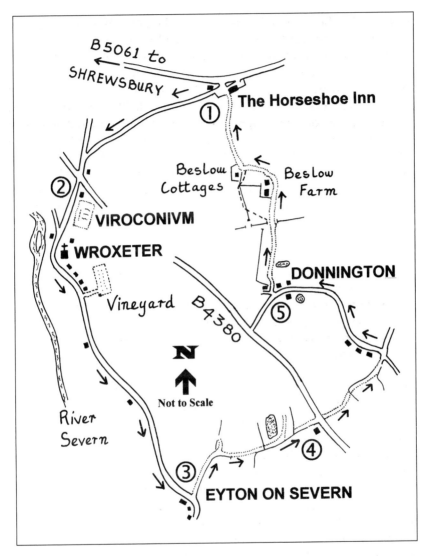

church of St Andrew prominently sited on the bend. The construction is mainly Norman but with traces of earlier Saxon work, and it incorporates some items from the old Roman town - note the pillars at the church gate. On reaching the last village house on the left the track going left leads to the Wroxeter Roman Vineyard. This is a working vineyard, open to the public, where the wines can be sampled and bought (by glass or bottle) and they also serve tea and coffee in the summer (telephone: 01743 761888). Go along the road for just over one mile, enjoying the splendid views to The Wrekin (left) and over the Severn Valley (right), towards the hamlet of Eyton on Severn, the location of a 'Point to Point' racecourse. Just past the first barns, on the right, turn left onto a stony, enclosed, track.

3. Follow the track and, as it opens into a field, keep to the right hedge, following it and then crossing an open section of field. Again join a hedge on the right, go through a bridlegate and continue along the hedge, passing a pond (left), to go through another bridlegate in the top right field corner (ignore the track sweeping left past the pond). Now follow the enclosed track to the B4380 and the site of The Watch Oak. This point was apparently the site of an oak tree, a 'look-out' place during the Civil War and also a watch point in coaching days. A plaque on the wall of the house gives more details.

4. Cross the road, go through a large gate, then follow the wide path up an open field as it sweeps left to go through another large gate; now follow the left fence. It is worth stopping to look back for a fine view over the Severn Valley. Continue along the left fence, join an enclosed track, then at a road junction turn left. Follow this country lane, past an imposing farmhouse, and then enjoy the view across the valley. Eventually reach the hamlet of Donnington then, by the post-box just past School House, turn right onto an enclosed gravel track.

5. Follow the track as it passes the house, then sweeps left and right, passes a pond and then reaches a wide gap in a hedge line. Ahead are the large barns of Beslow Farm and Riding Stables. At this point the official bridlepath goes diagonally left across the field, through the hedge and turns right, then back through the hedge by Beslow Cottages to rejoin the track. At the time of writing this section of path was not open but the landowner has provided a much easier permissive route along the track, around Beslow Farm and Stables, and on to Beslow Cottages where it rejoins the right of way. From there just follow the track back to the Horseshoe Inn.

LITTLE WENLOCK, THE WREKIN
THE HUNTSMAN

This walk leads to the summit of The Wrekin, from where you can see almost all of Shropshire, not to mention parts of Staffordshire, Worcestershire and Wales. There is also an imposing Iron Age hill fort to visit.

Situated in the shadow of The Wrekin is the village of Little Wenlock with its one pub, the Huntsman. This, now large, establishment started life as two small cottages built about 1900; these now form the spacious lounge area of the pub, complete with a large open fireplace and interesting prints of hunting scenes as well as an array of ornaments. At one time the cottages were altered to form the local police station and then eventually converted into a pub – this adds a whole new meaning to being 'called to the bar'. Since then the place has been considerably extended with a large restaurant area to the rear.

Being close to The Wrekin, the Huntsman caters for walkers. The bar snacks include such dishes as cod, scampi and home-made steak and kidney pie, alongside vegetarian specials such as Thai Red Vegetable Curry, Spicy Tomato Pasta and Vegetable Lasagne. In addition there is a full range of starters, main courses and sweets available in the restaurant. The main beers are Tetley and Bass and there is always a guest beer such as Flowers Original or Shropshire Lad. The lagers available are Carling and Carlsberg, the cider is Strongbow and, of course, there is Guinness. Food is available seven days a week from 12 noon to 2 pm (3 pm on Sundays) and 7 pm to 9 pm in the evening.

Telephone: 01952 505820.

- **HOW TO GET THERE:** Little Wenlock is located between Telford and The Wrekin, and is signposted from the A5223.
- **PARKING:** There is a large car park for customers at the side/rear of the pub. Please ask permission to leave your car there whilst you walk.
- **LENGTH OF THE WALK:** 6 miles. Map: OS Explorer 242 Telford, Ironbridge & The Wrekin (GR 648071).

THE WALK

1. On leaving the inn turn right, towards The Wrekin, and soon fork left (Spout Lane), signposted to Rushton and Garmston. Now enjoy a leisurely 2 mile walk along this quiet road with superb views across the Severn Valley to Brown Clee Hill, Wenlock Edge, Caer Caradoc and The Long Mynd. Soon this lane becomes part of the Shropshire Way (watch for the buzzard signs), which we follow over The Wrekin. Continue beyond the Scout Camp, then a house and farm, then encounter a wood (on the right). Ignore the first track into the wood, follow the lane gently uphill then, as a house comes into view ahead, turn right, via a gate, to enter the wood.

2. Follow the path into the wood (it is a right of way but the wood is private), ignoring numerous tracks going off to left and right. Keep to the well-trodden track (boot and hoof marks), with the route soon becoming narrow and steep as Little Hill is ascended. Follow the path over Little Hill, descend slightly then, as the wide track sweeps left, go straight ahead up the hill, quite steep in parts, to reach a prominent outcrop of rock called the Needle's Eye. The name derives from a large fissure in the rock, best viewed from its base, that is now blocked by rock falls.

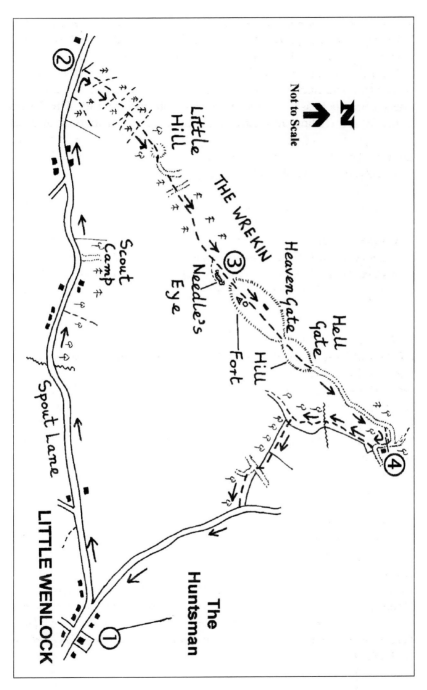

The Needle's Eye near the top of The Wrekin.

3. Continue through the entrance of the Iron Age hill fort (probably of the Cornovii tribe) to the summit where a toposcope gives details of the many places visible. This viewpoint shows the dramatic difference in the topography of Shropshire, from the hills of South Shropshire to the flat plain of North Shropshire, and is a spot worthy of a lingering visit. Continue over the top past the TV and radio mast (left) and then through two more hill fort entrances, known as Heaven Gate and Hell Gate. Now follow the wide track downhill (vehicles might be encountered) and continue on it as it sweeps right to a gate (prior to the gate, the Shropshire Way goes off to the left).

4. Continue past the gate and also Wrekin Cottage (on the left) then as the track sweeps left, continue ahead on a narrower track that goes gently uphill. Follow the track over a small stream and around several bends then, after fields appear on the left, look for a stile in the fence down to the left (located beyond a three-trunked tree). Follow the right fence line over more stiles to reach a track. Cross this and join another track, fence over to the left. Soon continue ahead on a narrower path, fence still over to the left, and on reaching a road go right and return to Little Wenlock.

WALK 6

COALPORT, NEAR TELFORD
THE WOODBRIDGE INN

This is a short and easy walk, but if you repeat it several times you will still find something new to discover on each occasion. The famous Coalport China Museum is a must for a visit. And, along the route, you will come across ample reminders that this is the area that gave birth to the Industrial Revolution.

At a strategic river crossing linking Coalport and Broseley, now spanned by a cast-iron bridge, stands the Woodbridge Inn, a strange name for a pub next to an iron bridge. The name gives the clue. The first Coalport Bridge, built here in 1780 was made of wood. This was damaged in the severe floods of 1795 and repaired using some cast-iron sections. The world's first major cast-iron bridge, built two miles upstream in 1779, had withstood the floods. Following more problems the Coalport Bridge was further repaired, using all cast-iron, in 1818 and that is the bridge in use today. The pub itself has also undergone many changes. Believed to have started life as a farm it then became an ale house, was once called Coalport House, then the Bridge Inn and now the Woodbridge Inn recalling the original wooden structure. It has recently had its own 'makeover' and now provides a warm, friendly bar with beams and brasses, and a large separate dining room. Outside there is a patio area, a large garden and an even larger river frontage, all with tables, where one can relax and watch the river flow by, ideal for their summer barbecues. If you enjoy it all enough you can even stay overnight as there are six en-suite rooms providing accommodation.

For the hungry and thirsty rambler there is an ample choice ranging through soups, spicy chicken wings, tiger prawns, home-made steak and kidney pie, Chicken Stilton, steaks, fish and curries. Add to this the 'daily specials' and the Sunday carvery and there is certainly enough to suit all tastes. The beer range includes John Smith's Cask Bitter, Tetley Bitter, Old Speckled Hen, guest beers and Guinness. There is also John Smith's Extra Smooth and Guinness Extra Cold as well as Carling, Foster's and Stella Artois lagers, Woodpecker and Strongbow ciders and a choice of wines. Food is available all week between 12 noon and 3 pm pm and from 6 pm to 9 pm and the pub is open all afternoon for drinks.
Telephone: 01952 882054.

- **HOW TO GET THERE:** The inn is at the Coalport Bridge over the River Severn and can be approached from either Coalport or Broseley.
- **PARKING:** There is a large car park at the pub for customers' use but please ask permission to leave your car there whilst you walk.
- **LENGTH OF THE WALK:** 2½ miles. Map: OS Explorer 242 Telford, Ironbridge & The Wrekin (GR 702020).

THE WALK
Note: Whilst this walk is mainly on surfaced roads and tracks the latter part, along the old Severn Valley Railway line (the Severn Way section), can become muddy after wet weather.

1. On leaving the pub walk to the road and turn right to cross the Coalport Bridge (originally named the Preens Eddy Bridge), thought to be the oldest cast-iron bridge in Britain still used for vehicular traffic. At the height of the Industrial Revolution, 200 years ago, the north river bank would have been devoid of trees and a hive of activity. Immediately over the bridge turn left and join the Silkin Way, a recreational path for walkers and cyclists, named after Lewis Silkin, the

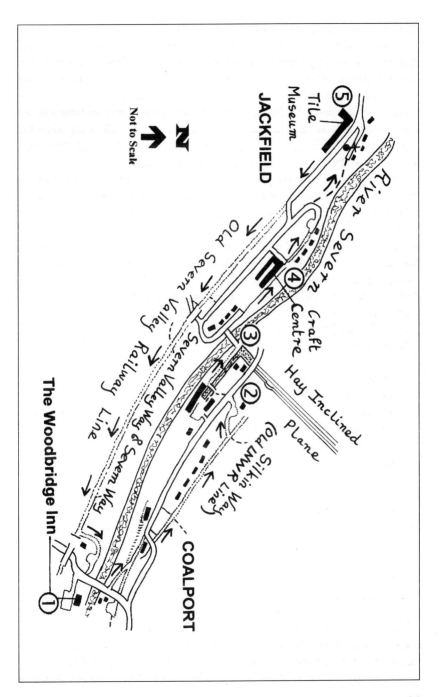

founder of the New Towns concept. The route, using disused rail lines and other paths, runs from Coalport to Bratton, just north of Wellington. After about 100 yards, by a path junction, stop and look directly ahead. The shallow ditch ahead is the remains of the old canal and the grassed area to the left of it was used to transfer goods from the canal to trows in the river; it is 'open access' and worth exploring. The Severn Trow was a flat-bottomed boat used to transport goods along the river. To continue the walk join another track and turn left, then go to the right of the cottage ahead. This is the route of the old London & North Western branch line linking Coalport to the main rail network, it opened in 1860 and closed in 1960. Go under the bridge (the pipe etc being installed after the rail line closed), pass the Brewery Inn car park and follow the track to a path junction about 100 yards past the last house on the left. Here turn left and follow that path (a link to the Severn Valley Way) to reach the road.

2. Cross the road and go to the left, entering the complex of the old Coalport China works which was in production between 1800 and 1926. The buildings have now been converted into a Youth Hostel complete with café, a gift shop and the China Museum, all worth visiting. At one time the canal, situated between the two main buildings, was used to bring in the raw materials and take out the finished products. When ready go to the restored section of canal and follow the towpath, which crosses over the canal, to reach the bottom of the Hay Inclined Plane, named after a local farm. This 'Plane', opened in 1793, transported 'tub' boats from the Shropshire Canal at Blists Hill, above, down to the canal on the river bank for loading onto the trows. By the bottom of the 'Plane' is the Tar Tunnel, cut in 1786 with the intention of giving a direct link from the Blists Hill mines to the river bank. However, a natural deposit of bitumen was discovered and this was commercially exploited into the mid 1800s. To continue the walk cross over the Jackfield Memorial Bridge.

3. This bridge was built in 1922 to serve as a memorial to those local people who died in the First World War; it was also very practical, as this free footbridge replaced a fare paying ferry. By 1999 it was in a very poor state so it was removed, and completely refurbished, in the spring of 2000, this with the support of the Heritage Lottery Fund. Once over, the route goes right to follow the lane, Ferry Road. However, first look at the Boat Inn – the door shows the various flood levels and inside

The Coalport Bridge by the Woodbridge Inn.

there are interesting photographs of the floods and old Jackfield. Proceed along the lane and soon join a track at the rear of the Maw & Co Encaustic Tile Works (now on the Severn Way, the long distance path that follows the River Severn from source to sea). Continue to the end of the building where the route is straight ahead on an enclosed path, but first turn left to the entrance to the Maws Craft Centre. The Maws factory, which once employed some 300 people, produced tiles from the early 1880s to about 1970. It now houses some 20 individual craft workshops and a café; worth seeing is the photograph on display at the entrance, taken by the RAF in 1948.

4. Having returned to the route follow the enclosed track, through an area known as Salthouses, to emerge at a large open area, once a pub car park. Continue ahead and, as the road turns left, take the narrow path on the right (the tarmac section is part of the old road that slid down the bank on the left). The path briefly joins the River Severn then emerges onto an intact section of the old road, Church Road, and then continues past Jackfield church, dedicated to St Mary the Virgin. Built in 1863 it used bricks of many different colours and the inside (the church is usually locked except for services) is partially tiled. Follow

33

the lane to a road junction, by Crossing Cottage, and turn left into Salthouse Road. Directly opposite is the old premises of the Craven Dunnill Tile Works which operated from about 1870 to 1950, employing some 100 people; it is now the Tile Museum.

5. Follow the road, with the tile works to the right, which is on the bed of the old Severn Valley Railway line (opened in 1862 and closed in the 1960s). In 1983 part of the old road (Church Road) collapsed, as we saw just now, due to a land slip, hence this realignment. As the road shimmies to the left keep straight ahead, still on the old rail line, now enclosed by trees. This is also part of the Severn Valley Way, another local walking and cycling route, which follows the old Severn Valley Railway between Coalport and Buildwas Power Station. Now simply enjoy this quiet track, passing the other side of Maws Tile Works and being joined by the Severn Way at a bridge over a road. Continue to where the path turns sharp left to drop down to the river and pass through the Preens Eddy Picnic Site (sounds like a great place to bring your teddy bear) then cross the road to the Woodbridge Inn.

CLAVERLEY, NEAR BRIDGNORTH
THE PLOUGH

This gentle walk begins at the beautiful village of Claverley, which has a wealth of historic buildings, including the Norman church of All Saints, with its superb 13th century wall paintings. The route passes through Shropshire countryside at its best and there are some wonderful panoramic views as well.

Claverley is a delightful village near the Staffordshire border (at the time of the Norman Conquest it was part of Staffordshire) with three pubs, a lovely old church and many timber-framed buildings. One such building is the Plough which is believed to have its origins in the 17th century, being built as a farmhouse. Today its cosy interior is full of nooks and crannies and there is a large open fire for the cold winter days and evenings. In addition there is a separate dining room, giving customers the choice of having a full restaurant meal or a substantial bar snack in one of the secluded alcoves, one being non-smoking.

The rambler can choose from a range of bar snacks including rolls and ploughman's lunches or have something from the main menu such as roast duck, minted chicken, beef and Guinness pie or local steaks, served plain or with a rich sauce. One of the 'House Specialities' is fish, delivered direct from Brixham, hence my own choice was grilled plaice, served with salad and vegetables, a substantial, but not too heavy meal before my walk. In addition there are daily specials to give an even wider choice of fare. The beers include Tetley Bitter, Ansells Mild and their own 'The Plough' Bitter (very good), brewed specially for the pub by the Enville Brewery. Lagers include Foster's and Stella Artois; there is also cider and Guinness and a wine list. Food is available on Monday to Saturday from 12 noon to 2 pm and 7 pm to 9 pm. On Sunday food is served between 12 noon and 2.30 pm.

Telephone: 01746 710365

1 **HOW TO GET THERE:** Claverley is situated some 5 miles due east of Bridgnorth. It is signposted from the A458 (Bridgnorth to Stourbridge) road and from the B4176 near its junction with the A454 (Bridgnorth to Wolverhampton) road.

1 **PARKING:** There is a large car park for customers at the side of the pub. Please advise the owner if leaving your car while you walk.

1 **LENGTH OF THE WALK:** 6 miles. Map: OS Explorer 218 Wyre Forest & Kidderminster (GR 794933).

THE WALK

1. From the pub front entrance turn right and walk towards the church, passing two more pubs and noticing the Old School House, the magnificent timber-framed Old Vicarage and the parish church of All Saints. If time permits a visit to the church is worthwhile, if only to see the c1200 wall paintings, in the style of the Bayeux Tapestry but thought to depict the Battle of the Virtues and Vices. The paintings were only uncovered in 1902 and are some of the most important of their kind in England.The church also has much more of interest and an explanatory booklet is available for a modest price. After the church continue the walk through the village, keep right at a fork in the road, pass a pond and stream on the right, then reach the point where the road goes sharply right. Here keep straight ahead, ascending a steep bank (via some rough cut steps) then go through a metal gate, in an electric fence, at the top.

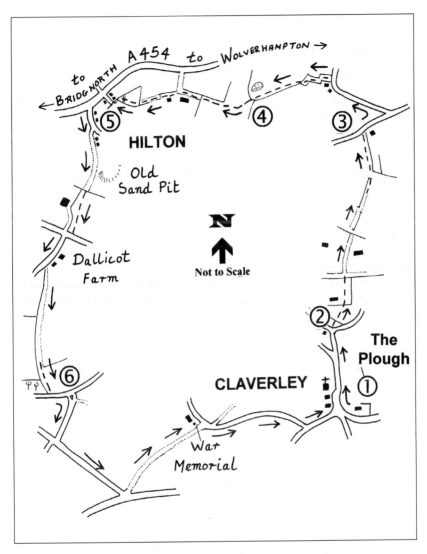

2. Now continue straight ahead over an open field to a stile to the right of a large chicken shed, to proceed through a tree plantation. If the chickens are out be prepared to be followed, quite an interesting experience. Exit the chicken farm via another metal gate and proceed directly ahead on a gravel track, passing another chicken shed on the right. Go through a gate (or use the stile) and keep ahead, following the field edge, initially the hedge is to the right but, after a gap, is then on

The church and Old Vicarage in Claverley village centre.

the left. Along this path there are panoramic views over south-eastern Shropshire and even a seat to sit and rest to admire the view. Keep the same direction, passing through another gap in the hedge and now following the fence on the right, then on reaching a lane turn right.

3. Follow the lane for about 250 yards and turn left at the next junction. Continue to a point just after the lane turns sharp right. Cross a stile on the left then walk through a paddock and zigzag around some stables. Follow the left fence to join a small, enclosed, section then cross two stiles to emerge into a field. From there follow the left field edge to a stile in the far left corner.

4. After crossing the stile walk straight into the arable field for about 150 yards, then turn right and walk towards the right end of a large barn, soon joining a fence on the right. Again this section of path offers sweeping views over the countryside. Pass the farm buildings to the left, and the farm shop, keep ahead to cross over a drive, then continue along the fence on the right. Pass a house, left, then join an enclosed path that leads to an open field. Go down the field to cross two stiles and proceed to the bottom left corner of the small field. Here again cross two stiles and follow a small enclosed path to another field and immediately turn right over a stile, now entering the hamlet of Hilton. Proceed to the A454 and turn left.

5. Go along the A454 for about 150 yards and turn left into Sandpit Lane then, after a further 150 yards, take the gravel track going off to the right. The gravel soon gives way to grass and proceeds gently uphill, the old sand pit being to the left, and now occupied by rabbits. Go through a kissing gate into an open field, pass a large house to the right, and proceed directly ahead to a stile to a lane. Here turn right and, almost immediately, turn left into another lane. Continue to a point just past a farm on the left, go through a large gate and follow the wide track, hedge to the right. Eventually reach woods on the right then, as the field edge sweeps left, cross a stile (on the right) to join a road and turn left.

6. Go along this lane, adorned with numerous wild flowers in spring and early summer, keep right at a fork then, at a road junction with a 'Private Drive' ahead, turn right. At the next road junction turn left (signposted to Claverley) then at another road junction turn sharp left, now on a wide dirt track, an old green lane. Along here the tower of Claverley church is visible ahead/right. Follow the track to the next junction by the war memorial and turn right along a tarmac lane. At the next junction turn left (note the old iron water pump opposite) and follow the road into Claverley village. At the village turn right to return to the Plough.

WALK 8

MUNSLOW
THE MUNSLOW INN

This is a wonderful walk along bridleways and field paths with sweeping views towards the hills of southern Shropshire, including the Clee Hills, High Vinnalls, Ragleth Hill and Hope Bowdler Hill. There is an optional, slightly longer route that will take you around Wenlock Edge.

Situated on the B4368 Morville to Craven Arms road, in the village of Munslow, is the imposing three-storey pub the Munslow Inn, formerly called the Crown. Precise details regarding the origin of the dwelling are unknown but it is believed to date back to the 16th century and to have been built for a local wealthy landowner. It is recorded that it was once the Hundred House where local courts were held for Munslow, and that it has been an inn (at one time a coaching stop) from the early 1700s. The position of the main dwelling door, up the steps, indicate that the area that is now the bars, dining room and brewery was

40

originally for storage. Today there are a mass of old beams visible, with a particularly large one above the fireplace in the main bar. And, if that is not enough, the pub also boasts a Micro-Brewery producing its own beer, has a secluded garden and does bed and breakfast. So this pub is an 'inn' in the full sense of the word.

A measure of the inn's popularity is that it attracts customers from a wide area, the quality of the food and drink being featured regularly in pub guides. Meals are prepared to order from fresh ingredients and local produce is used as much as possible. The choice ranges from simple bar snacks including filled baguettes, to a large variety of meals from the main menu or the daily specials board. Examples are Pan Seared Scallop Salad, Baked Seabass, Duxelles of Pork with mushroom and herb stuffing, as well as the usual steaks. I tried the Vegetarian Pasta Bolognese, with oodles of noodles topped with vegetables in a Bolognese sauce. For liquid refreshment the main beers are Shepherd Neame (Spitfire and Master Brew), as well as at least one of their own beers. The lager is Oranjeboom and there is also cider, Guinness and a small, but adequate, range of wines including some interesting ones from the Loire Valley. Food is available seven days a week from 12 noon to 2 pm and 7 pm to 9.30 pm.

Telephone: 01584 841205.

- **HOW TO GET THERE:** The village of Munslow is on the B4368 about halfway between Much Wenlock and Craven Arms.
- **PARKING:** There is a car park for customers across the road from the pub. Please advise the owners if leaving your car while you walk.
- **LENGTH OF THE WALK:** 4½ or 5½ miles, (please see the note at the start of the walk section). Map: OS Explorer 217 The Long Mynd & Wenlock Edge (GR 522874).

THE WALK

Note: The longer route, between points 2 and 3, particularly the descent towards Wetmoor Farm, can be muddy after wet weather. If conditions are, or have been, wet then the shorter route is recommended.

1. From the front entrance of the pub turn left and proceed to the war memorial by The Old School House, a former manor house. Turn left up the lane, follow it as it sweeps right, then at the next road junction turn left to reach St Michael's church, of mainly Norman construction

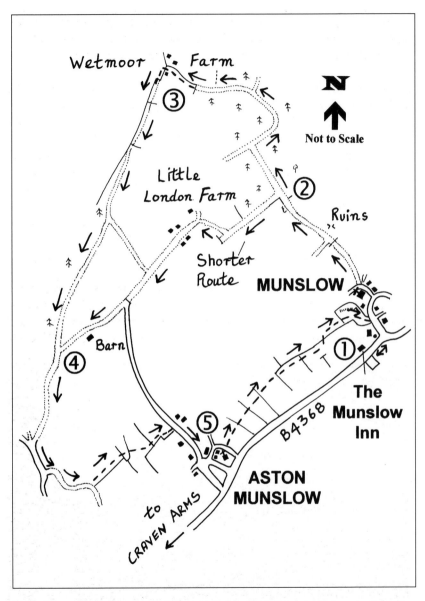

with some later additions. Continue past the church, keeping ahead as the lane sweeps left, to pass through a gate and join an old, sunken green lane, partly worn away to the bedrock by use and water erosion (care is needed here as the rocks can be slippery when wet). Proceed up the track, through a gate then past ruins on the right, to reach trees, also on the right. Just past a small old quarry, on the left, reach a track going off to the left – decision time, shorter or longer route.

2. Shorter route: Take the track going left, with woods again on the right, and a field to the left. Along this track, all the way to point 4, there is a splendid vista, left, across Corve Dale, to the two Clee Hills (Brown and Titterstone), and also towards High Vinnalls beyond Ludlow. The track soon opens up to another green lane then, at a path junction, gate ahead, you turn right. Follow the deeply rutted track (but with ample walking areas) as it meanders to join a gravel track, passes the buildings of Little London Farm, then joins a tarmac drive. As the drive joins a lane keep straight ahead, now on a gravel track, pass to the right of a large barn, cross an open field, then at a track junction turn left. Now see point 4 below to complete the walk.

   Longer route: Continue ahead, with trees either side, and at a T junction turn right. Follow the wide track as it sweeps left and starts to descend the north side of Wenlock Edge. This section can be muddy, depending on the time of year and use by horses (it is a bridlepath).

Aston Munslow church.

Eventually reach a gate, with the buildings of Wetmoor Farm visible ahead. Follow the right fence to another gate by the farm buildings, go through and turn left.

3. The route now follows the left fence to pass through a bridlegate and join another green lane. As the route climbs higher, going through more gates and then reaching a wood to the left, a vista opens up, right, across Ape Dale looking towards Church Stretton. The main hills visible are that of Ragleth, Hazler and Hope Bowdler, the high plateau of The Long Mynd being hidden behind Ragleth Hill. Follow the track back to the top of Wenlock Edge and at a path junction keep right, with trees to the right and an open field to the left. The view here is now across Corve Dale, with a superb view of both Brown Clee Hill and Titterstone Clee Hill. Continue on the track as it sweeps gently left and is then joined by a track coming from a large barn on the left.

4. Both routes: Follow the wide track downhill, drinking in the view across Corve Dale, and join a lane. After about 200 yards, as the lane is sweeping right, take a track on the left. Continue on this track, around several bends, for some 400 yards to cross a stile on the left. Follow the right fence/hedge to cross two stiles and then go part right, down the field, to a gate to the left of a large tree. Now follow the right fence to a lane, turn right, and follow the lane into Aston Munslow, with its interesting old buildings, particularly the medieval White House.

5. At the road junction in the village turn left and then, after the last house on the right, turn right up an unmade lane. Just past the small church cross a stile on the left and continue ahead across arable fields. The route is now almost a straight line across several open fields. Cross a stile at a hedge corner and now follow the left hedge. After two fields, cross a stile on the left. Maintain the same direction, fence now on the right, and pass a graveyard of old cars and farm implements. Cross the stile in the field corner, first keep ahead and then sweep gently right, keeping the steep slope downwards to your left. Eventually reach the far corner of the field, cross a stile and footbridge to reach the lane, then turn right to retrace your steps back past the war memorial to return to the inn.

SHATTERFORD
THE RED LION INN
❧❀❧

The pub is especially good here and you may be tempted to linger awhile. Do leave time for the walk, though, because it is one of delightful contrasts. There is the farming hamlet of Romsley, a secluded dingle, some woodland and an ancient green lane.

The Red Lion Inn is situated just on the Shropshire border with Worcestershire, it even has a Worcestershire postal address, Shatterford, and at first glance it seems an isolated stretch of road for an inn. Old maps show the reason. Built in 1835 and registered as a 'Beer House' in the same year, it is situated on the main route between Kidderminster and Bridgnorth (now the A442) and at the crossroads of a route from the then river ferry at Upper Arley through to Romsley and then on to Kinver. Being located in this prime position it was subsequently bought by the Kidderminster Brewery in 1897 and then went through several company takeovers to eventually become a free house in 1985. A framed pub history is on display in the main bar and is worth reading.

Over the years the Red Lion Inn has built up a regular clientele because of its good atmosphere and excellent beer and food. There are two bars, one non-smoking, and also a large restaurant at the rear. The choice of food ranges from bar snacks, such as sandwiches and baked potatoes, to a full à la carte menu, everything from a 'chip butty' to a gourmet meal. A speciality is fresh fish, delivered daily, and there is always a range of specials. My own choice was Shropshire Venison from the Clee Hills, provided by a butcher in Ludlow, served with a green peppercorn sauce and a separate dish of vegetables. The normal range of beers includes Banks's Mild and Bitter, Bathams Bitter (wonderful) and guests such as Marston's Pedigree and Shropshire Lad. The lagers are Harp and Foster's and the cider is Strongbow; there is also Guinness and a good wine list. Food is available seven days a week, from 12 noon to 2 pm at lunchtime, and in the evening from 6.30 pm to 9.30 pm (10 pm on Friday and Saturday and 7 pm to 9.30 pm on Sunday).

Telephone: 01299 861221.

- **HOW TO GET THERE:** The Red Lion Inn is on the A442 some 5 miles north of Kidderminster.
- **PARKING:** In the 'overflow' car park (patrons only) at the Worcestershire side of the pub.
- **LENGTH OF THE WALK:** 5 miles. Map: OS Explorer 218 Wyre Forest & Kidderminster (GR 779823).

THE WALK

1. Walk up the lane alongside the inn, the view opening up to the left being the Clee Hills. At the junction turn left and follow the road for some 500 yards and just past a house on the left, The Highlands, turn right into a narrow lane. Follow the narrow lane, turn left at the T junction, continue past farm buildings and, at the next road junction, turn sharp right. Follow the country lane downhill then, just prior to a brook, turn left over a stile.

2. The route now follows Bowhills Dingle; the brook is to the right but only visible for part of the walk. From the stile continue ahead to negotiate a small stream, aided by some useful stones, then go up the bank to cross a stile and turn right. Continue to another stile and then through old coppice woodland to reach a footbridge (local historians

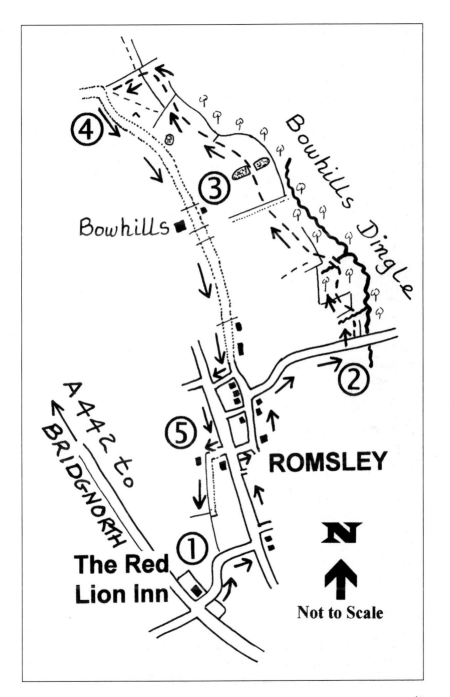

Bowhills

Bowhills Dingle

ROMSLEY

A 442 to
BRIDGNORTH

The Red
Lion Inn

N

Not to Scale

believe there was once a mill here). Go up the bank to cross another stile and turn right. The route is now across pasture land, generally diverging from the trees to the right, to cross another stile; from there continue to the central dam between two ponds. (The official footpath is now different to that shown on the older maps.)

3. From the central dam keep straight ahead across open pasture to eventually reach the tree line, a stile here is on the line of a fence, now removed. Keep in the same general direction, skirting trees and scrubland, to reach a stile in the far right corner of the field (ignore the stile in the same fence but to the left). Now cross a long, narrow field to eventually reach the far left corner. Cross, or go around, the stile and go straight up the field (ignoring the stile immediately on the right), following the fence/hedge on the right. At the top join an old green lane and turn left.

4. The route now follows this old lane, a bridleway, with many opportunities to stop and admire the views. To the right, at gaps in the hedge, the view is across the Severn Valley to the Clee Hills; the lake visible to the north is Chelmarsh Reservoir. To the left the view is across Bowhills Dingle, the route just walked, and beyond that to Staffordshire and Kinver Edge. Proceed along the lane to pass the ruins of an old barn, then go through the farmyard of Bowhills to eventually pass another farm and reach a tarmac lane, now back in Romsley. Here turn right and at the next T junction turn left, then follow the road for some 400 yards to turn down a gravel track on the right.

5. Follow the gravel track and, just prior to a gate, turn left, joining an old green lane. Follow the enclosed path to a stile, cross and turn left to follow the left fence. On a clear day the view from here, both down and across the Severn Valley, includes the Malvern, Abberley and Clee Hills. At the road turn right and follow it back to the Red Lion Inn.

WALK 10

ANGELBANK, NEAR CLEEHILL
THE ROYAL OAK

This is an excellent ramble that takes you across the lower slopes of Titterstone Clee Hill with superb panoramic views over Corve Dale to Wenlock Edge and the Stretton Hills, over the Onny Valley to The Long Mynd, and down the Teme Valley towards Wales. You can add to this some industrial archaeology (two inclined planes), an attractive village (Bitterley) and a visit to Bedlam – an interesting outing indeed.

Titterstone Clee Hill has been mined and quarried for coal and stone for centuries, the major product of the quarries being 'dhu' (black) stone, a rock formed from dark basaltic lava and used extensively in road building. This, in turn, required buildings to provide homes and the provision of food and drink for the workers and their families. One such building is the Royal Oak, its origin is uncertain but the older parts are believed to date from the 18th century, the premises then expanding in the mid 19th century with the increased quarrying. To withstand the cold wind that can sweep the hill in winter the construction is thick, solid stone, and it was recorded as once being a slaughterhouse and butcher's as well as an ale house. Today its thick walls provide warmth in winter and coolness in summer, but the inside now has a 'dining' lounge and also a bar with a large games area. In addition there is a function room for groups (such as Rambling Clubs), an outside sheltered patio and a large garden.

Whilst being on the main A4117 provides some passing trade this pub has to rely on attracting regular clientele from a larger area by providing quality food and good service. Accordingly the lunchtime menu ranges from sandwiches and baguettes through to meals such as mixed grill, steaks and curries with additional dishes in the evening. On Sundays there are also the traditional roast dishes. For liquid refreshment the beer range includes Boddingtons Bitter, Tetley Bitter and regular guests such as Hydes' Anvil of Manchester; there is also Murphy's Irish Stout. The lagers are Heineken and Stella Artois, the ciders are Scrumpy Jack, Strongbow and Woodpecker and there is also a selection of wines. Food is available from 12 noon to 3 pm and 6.30 pm to 9.30 pm all week.

Telephone: 01584 890485.

- **HOW TO GET THERE:** The Royal Oak is situated on the A4117 about one mile west of Cleehill village.
- **PARKING:** There is a large car park for customers at the side of the pub. Please ask permission before leaving your car.
- **LENGTH OF THE WALK:** 6 miles. Map: OS Explorer 203 Ludlow, Tenbury Wells & Cleobury Mortimer (GR 581758).

THE WALK

1. On leaving the front entrance of the pub turn left, follow the A4117 for 100 yards then turn left up a farm track. Continue through the farmyard, through a gate to an enclosure, then over a stile to a field. Continue ahead to a tarmac lane and turn left, following the lane around a bend for about 100 yards then, as the lane then sweeps left, turn right up a house drive (bridlegate and cattle grid). This section of route is now on the Shropshire Way, identified by the buzzard symbol. Follow the gravel drive and where the track divides (cattle grid to the left) keep straight ahead, across the bottom of a garden, to enter a field via a gate. Now go part left and diagonally across the field to the far left

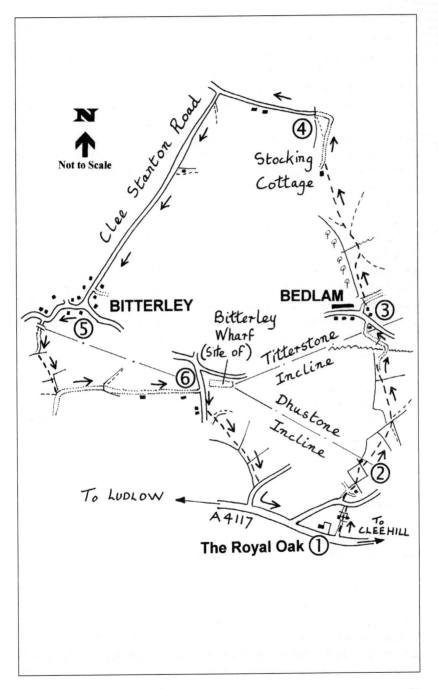

corner, Titterstone Clee Hill directly ahead. Go through a gate, passing a cottage on the left, across the gravel farmyard and over a causeway across a deep cutting. This cutting is the line of the Dhustone Incline, built in 1862 to convey the stone from the quarry to Bitterley Wharf, then on to Ludlow and the main Shrewsbury/Hereford rail link.

2. Proceed directly across the field towards Titterstone Clee Hill, with a view opening up, left, towards Corve Dale, the Onny Valley and the hills beyond, including The Long Mynd. Cross a stile in a fence, go slightly left and reach a gate in the far left corner of the next field. Once through cross over a small brook and immediately turn left, now leaving the Shropshire Way. Proceed ahead over a large field, there is no defined path but aim for a group of houses – Bedlam – across the valley. Cross a stile in a fence and move towards the left fence line. Join an old green lane and follow it as it sweeps downwards to cross Benson's Brook and rise again, through an old iron gate, then between two stone walls, to reach the hamlet of Bedlam. The high stone walls mark the line of the Titterstone Incline that carried stone down from a quarry near the summit, joining with the Dhustone Incline at Bitterley Wharf. The hamlet of Bedlam is called Titterstone on some OS maps, but locally is signposted as Bedlam, possibly from the noise that emanated from the quarry and the Incline.

3. Turn left at the tarmac lane and almost immediately sweep right onto a gravel/stony track. (A short detour along the lane reveals the war memorial and a view towards Ludlow and the Teme Valley.) Follow the stony track as it sweeps around to reach two adjacent gates. Once through (your choice) immediately turn left, cross a small stream, then generally follow the left tree line over rough moorland, Titterstone Clee Hill to the right. Keep generally parallel to the left tree line, through high bracken in summer or autumn, a choice of narrower tracks eventually sweeping around a dip to join a wider track. Follow this to cross a small brook and then take the left fork as the track splits. Soon the track starts to descend, the tree line to the left drops away (ignore a narrow track towards the trees) and a panoramic view opens up. Ahead/right is Brown Clee Hill with the two radio masts, ahead is Corve Dale and Wenlock Edge, ahead/left is the ridge of The Long Mynd whilst to the left are the Clun and Teme Valleys with Wales beyond. The path now slowly descends to pass Stocking Cottage (on the left) and a drive is joined which is followed to reach a tarmac lane.

4. Go along the lane passing Bank Farm (on the left) and at a road junction turn left. This road (Clee Stanton Road) is now followed for about 1½ miles to reach the village of Bitterley. The road is generally quiet (over several visits only horses were encountered) and in summer the banks are a profusion of wild flowers and butterflies. On reaching Bitterley turn right at the road junction, signposted to Ludlow. The present siting of the village, away from the church, apparently occurred in the 17th century, to locate people away from the vicinity of Bitterley Court.

5. Follow the meandering road towards Ludlow, noting some of the old buildings and ornate chimneys. After passing Lower Court (on the right) proceed around a right-hand bend and then, just prior to barns on the right, take a stony track going left. Pass under an old railway bridge (the old line between Bitterley Wharf and Ludlow) and enter an old green lane. Follow this enclosed track as it meanders upwards, enters a large field, then sweeps right to another gate. Now follow the left hedge (with a view towards Ludlow and High Vinnalls to the right) and on reaching a track turn left. Follow this track, first enclosed then along a field edge, past a farm building (on the right) and then a cottage (note the ornate stone structure, possibly an old folly). On reaching a lane turn right.

6. Go up the lane for just over 100 yards then go through a gate on the left, opposite a farm. (This path is not part of the Shropshire Way but when researched some Shropshire Way markers had been used.) Now go part right, across the field, to a stile by a gate, then proceed diagonally across the next field to a stile in the far corner. Follow the right hedge/fence to another (possibly awkward) stile and again follow the right hedge to enter a lane. Here turn right, reach the A4117, turn left and follow the pavement, uphill, back to the Royal Oak.

WALK 11

LLANFAIR WATERDINE, NEAR KNIGHTON THE WATERDINE

This walk begins at the banks of the River Teme and passes over Llanfair Hill to visit the great earthwork of Offa's Dyke. From there, and on the return route, you will have some superb views over South-West Shropshire

Llanfair Waterdine (the church by the water) was once, as the name implies, in Wales but today this very small village lies just inside Shropshire, the national boundary now being the River Teme. At the western end of the village is the church (Saint Mary's, rebuilt in 1854) and the village pub, now the Waterdine but until early 2000 called the Red Lion. Close by is Everest Hall, once the village school but now the village hall, so named because Sir John Hunt, conqueror of Everest, was a local parishioner. The Waterdine, thought to have been built in 1562

54

as a drovers' inn, has undergone many alterations and improvements over the years to become what it is today, a restaurant and inn complete with en-suite accommodation. Timbers from the old barn which once occupied the parking area and was demolished in the 1940s were used in the renovations. This attractive hostelry now has a lounge bar, a non-smoking lounge, a separate dining room, a dining conservatory and a secluded garden that overlooks the Teme Valley.

People seeking refreshment will be equally impressed with the range of food available, from ploughman's lunches with a choice of cheese, to spicy sausage as well as various beef, lamb, duck and vegetarian dishes – my own choice of Cornish Crab Salad was a work of art as well as tasting good. The evening menu includes such gastronomic delights as Roast Pigeon Breast and Lobster Thermidor (the lobsters being delivered live to the premises). For real ale drinkers there are beers such as Dorothy Goodbody's or Jack Snipe from Woodhampton; there is also Tetley Smoothflow Bitter as well as Guinness, Strongbow cider and a choice of Carling or Bitburger lager. Being a restaurant it has an extensive wine list. Food is available at lunchtimes, except Mondays, from 12 noon to 2 pm and every evening from 7 pm to 9 pm.

Telephone: 01547 528214.

- **HOW TO GET THERE:** From Knighton (the location of the Offa's Dyke Centre) take the B4355 going west (signposted to Beguildy), pass by Knucklas to reach Lloyney then turn right to cross the River Teme. Once over the bridge turn left to eventually reach the inn.
- **PARKING:** There is a small car park opposite the inn (could be full when the church is in use). Please advise the owner if leaving your car while you walk.
- **LENGTH OF THE WALK:** 6 miles. Map: OS Explorer 201 Knighton & Presteigne (GR 241762).

THE WALK

1. On leaving the Waterdine turn right and follow the road past Everest Hall. Continue past houses and take the next turning left (to Black Hall), following this attractive country lane for about one mile, keeping left at a fork in the road. (The lane going right is to Black Hall which is now visible ahead/right.) Continue past the first group of dwellings ignoring the bridleway going right and then, just prior to a barn and ruined building, turn sharp right up a stony track to a gate.

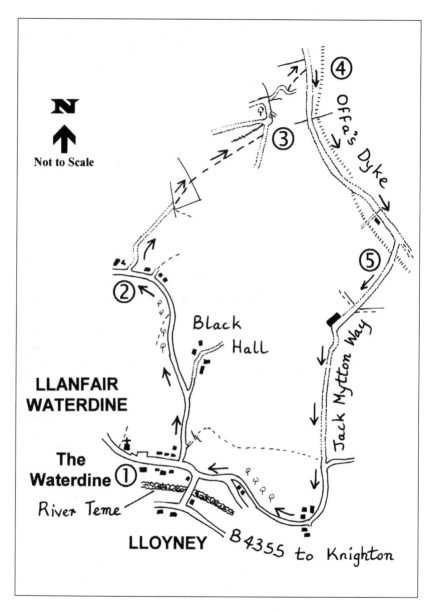

2. Now the serious uphill walk begins, following a wide track that meanders upwards to eventually reach a gate to a field. (Frequent stops should be made to look back over the Teme Valley into Wales!) Once in the field go part left (no visible path) and reach a bridlegate in the far fence. Go through and continue ahead, keeping parallel to the valley on the left and generally following the contour line – a good aiming point is just to the right of the trees at the head of the valley. Eventually reach a wide track and here turn left.

3. Initially go slightly downhill and at a track junction keep ahead, now going uphill again. (Notice the interesting, many trunked, tree on the left.) Continue to another path junction and turn right through a gate. Here the OS map shows the path as going part left and across the hill to a gate in the far fence, but this is not visible on the ground. The best route is to follow a track that winds its way uphill, going left, right and again left. After the second left sweep turn left, off the track, and follow the contour around the side of the hill to eventually reach the gate in the far fence. (If this turn is missed – not marked and not immediately noticeable – continuing ahead will lead to the fence; here turn left and follow it until the gate is reached.) Go through the gate and turn right. This wide track is the Jack Mytton Way, Offa's Dyke is over to the left.

4. Initially the route follows the Jack Mytton Way, a 70 mile bridleway from Highley, by the River Severn, to Llanfair Waterdine, by the River Teme. It is named after 'Mad Jack' Mytton (1796–1834), a squire from northern Shropshire and one time MP for Shrewsbury, who was known for his horsemanship and drinking. This part of the walk also passes one of the best sections of Offa's Dyke, with the western ditch being well preserved. After some 400 yards there is a choice of path, the Dyke or the track, the Dyke giving a better viewpoint as it is higher. On this walk over Llanfair Hill the view, to the left is over Shropshire, to the right it is across the Teme Valley into Wales. On rejoining the track proceed in the same direction, pass a barn on the right and continue on the stony track as it turns right to pass through the Dyke.

5. It is now a case of following the Jack Mytton Way (watch for the blue horse and rider waymark discs) as it winds downhill with superb views across the Teme Valley to the hills of Wales. After almost 1½ miles a narrow lane is reached. Ignore the bridleway going off to the right (this is a possible route back but can be very muddy in wet conditions) and continue along the road to then turn right between farm buildings. Again keep ahead at the next road junction and at another junction go right. Now follow the lane back to Llanfair Waterdine and the pub.

WALK 12

NEWCASTLE ON CLUN
THE CROWN INN

This is border country and here is a shortish walk, taking you above Folly Brook to visit an extremely well preserved section of Offa's Dyke. There are panoramic views, especially on a clear day.

Newcastle on Clun lies at what was a strategic crossroads as the ancient hill fort above it testifies. The Clun Valley goes east to west and there is a route from the Kerry Ridgeway coming along the Folly Valley and then continuing south, over Llanfair Hill, to Llanfair Waterdine. The 'new' castle of the name was probably the one by the bank of the River Clun, only a mound now remains. Situated on the B4368 is the Crown Inn. Its oldest parts, the lounge bar and dining room, are late 17th century, the public bar area was built in the mid 19th century and the games room was added in the early 20th century. Recorded as being a drovers' inn, on the route along the Clun Valley, it still has its old exposed beams, is a local meeting place and provides a warm welcome, with accommodation, to travellers visiting the area.

This is an inn that prides itself on its selection of 'real ales' including Greene King IPA and Abbot Ale, alongside regular guests – for example, from Jennings, a Cumbria brewery. Also available are Tetley Bitter, Ansells Mild, Guinness, Carlsberg lager, Strongbow and Woodpecker ciders, plus a selection of wines. In keeping with an inn that provides accommodation there is a good choice of food ranging from simple bar snacks through to a full meal. Included are dishes such as lasagne, tagliatelle, Pork in Creamy Cider, Cajun Chicken, Devilled Chicken, Mexican Meatballs, grilled steaks (with a selection of mustards) and a range of puddings. Food is usually available every day from 12 noon to 2 pm and in the evenings from 7 pm to 9.30 pm (9 pm on Sunday).

Telephone: 01588 640271.

- **HOW TO GET THERE:** Newcastle is located 4 miles west of Clun on the B4368.
- **PARKING:** There is limited parking for customers at the side of the pub – please advise the owners if leaving your car while you walk.
- **LENGTH OF THE WALK:** 4½ miles. Maps: OS Explorer 201 Knighton & Presteigne and 216 Welshpool & Montgomery (GR 248823).

THE WALK

1. Leaving the front entrance of the pub turn right, follow the B4368 to a crossroads and continue ahead on a minor road. Go past Newcastle Hall and all the farm buildings then turn right, up a wide gravel track (Newcastle Court) to pass more buildings and sweep left. Almost immediately after the turn take the right fork going uphill through trees, the Folly Valley to the left. This wide track is now followed to a gate which leads to open hillside, the view being up the Folly Valley, ahead/left. Continue past the ruins of some old barns (Upper Barn) and then, as the more prominent track turns right into a field, keep straight ahead, following the right hedge/fence to a stile and gate. Continue on a grassy track with trees on the left, enter a field and follow the right hedge to join a road and turn right.

2. The route is now along this country lane, going gently downhill with fine views over the hilly terrain of South-West Shropshire (the ridge on the left is Mount Bank). Ignore the stile on the left. Also, the road provides a superb view of Offa's Dyke which comes into view – generally ahead – as a quite distinct line going across the hillside, its route being more visible from here than when walking on it. It does

show, however, what a prominent feature in the landscape it must have been when first constructed over 1,200 years ago. Follow the road down to a junction and turn left, the Dyke now up on the right, and continue until reaching buildings on the right (Bridge Farm). Here turn right into the drive then go straight ahead, through a gate, onto a track.

3. After only 50 yards from this gate turn sharp right up a track, then keep straight ahead as the more prominent track sweeps left. The next mile is now on the Offa's Dyke Path, the key is to watch out for the acorn symbol on the stiles. On this section the Dyke is more an enhancement of the natural land slope than a distinct mound, a contrast to the section used in Walk 11. It does, however, give wonderful views over the

The Clun Valley from the Offa's Dyke Path.

countryside, ahead and to the right. Part way along, by a spring, is a section that can be muddy after wet weather - the best route here is to go down the Dyke and ascend again when past the boggy ground. The local sheep have been helpful in providing tracks for this purpose.

4. Follow the Dyke over several stiles, at one point descending very steeply through larch trees, the angle of the trees showing the strength and direction of the prevailing wind. After a slight uphill section the path descends again towards the Clun Valley, with Newcastle coming into view to the right. Directly ahead, across the valley, the Dyke rises up the hillside, its route distinguished by a straight line of trees. On reaching a track at the bottom of this gentle slope do not cross the stile ahead but turn right, through a gate, to reach a road.

5. Go down the road to a junction, turn right and follow that road back to Newcastle, passing the relatively modern (mid 19th century) church of St John the Evangelist with its unusual lychgate (worth going through to try it then exit the churchyard at the far side). Continue along Church Road into Newcastle and take the first road on the left, following this as it sweeps right to return to the Crown Inn.

CRAVEN ARMS
THE STOKESAY CASTLE INN

There is plenty to interest everyone here. Allow time for a visit to the 13th century fortified manor house of Stokesay Castle which you will pass en route. The pub at the beginning of the walk is excellent and the combination offers a marvellous day's outing.

Craven Arms, the name deriving from the 'coat of arms' awarded to Lord Craven of Stokesay Castle in the 17th century, is at the junction of two old trade routes – the north/south route (now the A49) and the east/west route (now the B4368). The north/south route was also a coaching route linking Chester and Bristol, resulting in the building, in 1896, of what is now the Stokesay Castle Inn. At that time paying passengers stayed at the Craven Arms Hotel and the coachmen and the horses stayed at another inn (now demolished). It is said that the locals objected to the smell of the horses (and possibly the coachmen) so this new inn was built for the express purpose of stabling the horses and accommodating the coachmen. Today the inn still provides accommodation, now for ramblers visiting this beautiful part of the world. An added attraction is the adjacent Shropshire Hills Discovery Centre (allow two hours for a full visit). For its information line, telephone: 01588 676040.

One advantage of starting a walk from this inn is the flexible opening times. Food is available all day from 10 am to 9 pm, ranging from breakfast or morning coffee through to a wide range of bar snacks including baguettes and jacket potatoes. There is also a menu of starters and main courses such as soup, pâté and garlic mushrooms, then Steak in Ale Pie, Lambs Liver and Bacon, Ham, Egg and Chips and so on. The main beer range is Banks's (including Banks's Original and Banks's Bitter) and Marston's Pedigree, with regular guests. Three lagers are on offer, Harp, Foster's and Kronenbourg 1664, and the cider is Strongbow. There is also a comprehensive wine list. In the evening an additional à la carte menu is available from 6.30 pm to 9 pm.

Telephone: 01588 672304.

- **HOW TO GET THERE:** The Stokesay Castle Inn is located in School Road, off the A49, at the southern end of Craven Arms (adjacent to the Shropshire Hills Discovery Centre).
- **PARKING:** At the side and rear of the inn; there are also 12 parking places allocated to inn customers at the Discovery Centre. Please advise the owners if leaving your car while you walk.
- **LENGTH OF WALK:** 4 miles. Map: OS Explorer 217 The Long Mynd & Wenlock Edge (GR 435826).

THE WALK

1. From the inn entrance turn left and pass the Shropshire Hills Discovery Centre, specifically designed to give people information on the natural beauty of South Shropshire (a visit is recommended). Cross the A49 and continue up a track, Dodds Lane, pass under the railway line and at the end cross a stile to a field. Follow the left hedge (Stoke Wood is ahead/left) to another stile, cross the field to the far side to enter trees, passing a ruined cottage on the right. Go through a gate, turn right, then follow the right hedge through three fields (in the third field the diagonal track to the left is a short cut but the field edge path gives better all round views). Continue to the top right-hand corner of the third field, turn left and join a wide track.

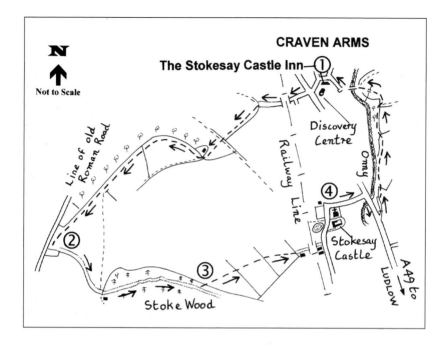

2. Follow the track, the right of way, with a fine view to the left across Craven Arms to the hills around Church Stretton, also up Ape Dale and the western end of Wenlock Edge. On reaching a house (on the right) continue on the wide track which now enters Stoke Wood, following it for about 700 yards to reach a narrow track going off to the left. This narrow path could be missed so watch for fields being just visible through the trees then take the path going downwards, with conifer trees on the left, to reach a stile.

3. Once in the field go slightly right and walk directly towards Stokesay Castle, enjoying the splendid views left and ahead. Starting from the left the hills visible are The Long Mynd, then sweeping right to Caer Caradoc and Hope Bowdler Hill; directly behind Stokesay Castle is Nortoncamp Wood. Proceed across two fields and in the third field continue slightly right to reach a gate by a large tree. Follow the path to meet a railway crossing gate. Go through this gate but don't forget to stop, look and listen before crossing the railway line. Continue to a lane and turn left. Stokesay Castle is now ahead, the pond to the left originally supplying the water for the moat. The 'Castle' is actually a fortified manor house dating mainly from the 13th century and is well worth visiting. Over its life it has had many owners and tenants, most of

The Shropshire Hills Visitor Centre.

the building as seen now dating from the time of Lawrence of Ludlow, a prosperous wool merchant who obtained the tenancy for the price of a 'juvenile sparrow hawk'. Today the premises are administered by English Heritage; for opening times, telephone: 01588 672544. Adjacent is the little church of St John the Baptist, which had 12th century origins but was rebuilt in the 17th century.

4. On leaving the 'Castle' follow the lane around to the A49, turn right, cross over the Onny (good view of the weir) and about 150 yards beyond the bridge cross the A49 (by a road junction sign) to take a tarmac track going down to the left, a section of the old A49. At the end of the track go down steps on the right then cross a small field to follow the bank of the River Onny. The path then goes gently uphill, above the river, fence on the left. At the field corner cross the stile and continue ahead, fence now on the right and steep slope to the left. At the next stile cross and turn left, fence again on the left, and soon start to sweep left. Cross a footbridge over a small stream and then proceed across the field to a gated iron footbridge over the River Onny. Follow the path to a road that goes to the right and at the next road junction turn left to reach the Stokesay Castle Inn.

LYDBURY NORTH
THE POWIS ARMS

This is a great walk to appreciate the rolling hills of South-West Shropshire. The routes takes you around the slopes of Oakeley Mynd giving superb views over the Onny Valley towards The Long Mynd, across the upper Camlad Valley to Heath Mynd and Corndon Hill then finally towards Bishop's Castle and Blakeridge Wood.

The old village of Lydbury North (recorded in the Domesday Book) is today associated with Walcot Hall, originally built by the Walcot family but subsequently owned by Robert, Lord Clive, of India. His stepson, became the Earl of Powis and it is from that title, not the Welsh county, that the Powis Arms takes its name. (When the estate was owned by the Earls of Powis the pub closed at 8 pm to ensure the workers went to bed early.) This large, Georgian hostelry has quite an interesting history, being built as a coaching inn (on the east/west route through Bishop's Castle and Craven Arms) about the late 18th century. Originally called the New Inn it was also the Parish Room (for holding meetings and collecting rents) as well as an inn. Today it has two bars, a games room and a separate dining room, the old Parish Room until the mid 1900s. The upstairs area provides overnight accommodation and at the rear there is a garden and facilities for touring caravans and tents.

Food is available here from 12 noon to 2 pm on Tuesday to Sunday and from 7 pm to 9 pm every evening. Dishes range from simple bar snacks such as sandwiches and fish and chips to a fuller menu of starters (for example, calamari, soup, feta cheese and leek tart), main courses (grilled plaice, rump steak and a vegetarian selection, among others) and desserts – my own lunchtime choice of a hand-carved beef salad was very substantial. The main beers are Tetley Bitter plus one beer from the Six Bells Brewery at Bishop's Castle, as well as a guest such as Hereford Pale Ale from the Wye Valley Brewery. There is also Ansells Mild, Carlsberg lager, Guinness and ciders (Strongbow and Weston's) as well as a list of wines from around the world. Plenty of choice for a thirsty rambler.

Telephone: 01588 680254.

- **HOW TO GET THERE:** The Powis Arms is situated on the B4385 some 3 miles south-east of Bishop's Castle.
- **PARKING:** There is a customers' car park at the rear of the inn; please advise staff if leaving your car while you walk.
- **LENGTH OF THE WALK:** 6 miles. Map: OS Explorer 216 Welshpool & Montgomery (GR 349859).

THE WALK

1. From the front of the pub turn right and follow the B4385 past the parish church of St Michael and All Angels, of mainly 12th century construction. Take the next lane left after the church and follow it (ignore the left fork) to a junction and turn right. Just prior to the cottage at the end of the lane turn left onto a footpath (this may be overgrown for the first few yards but it soon opens out into an old green lane). Follow this ancient sunken track as it meanders and ascends the hill to pass to the left of a small quarry area (the reason for the old lane). Just past the quarry area the path emerges to fields on the left; do not enter that field (an alternative route from Lydbury North) but continue ahead, and slightly right, to a stile to another field.

2. Follow the left field edge as it continues upwards, crossing another

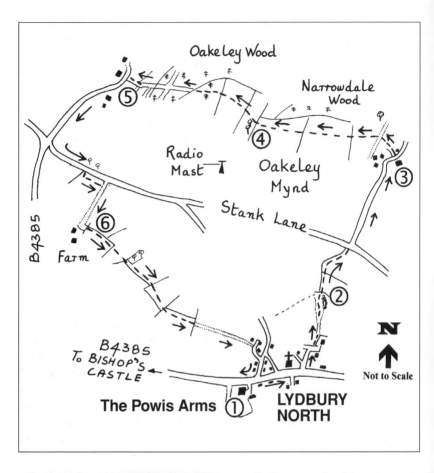

stile then sweeping right alongside a wood. Soon reach a lane via a gate (Stank Lane), cross it and continue along the narrow road opposite with a good view, right, of The Long Mynd and, in the far distance, Brown Clee Hill. Soon the road descends and sweeps right then, at the bottom, you turn left to cross a stile opposite a black and white timber-framed cottage.

3. From the stile go up to the open field, then go part left to a stile in the far hedge (located about midway between barns on the left and a large tree to the right). Now cross a farm drive and again go slightly left to cross another field to a stile in the opposite hedge. At this point the view looking back is across the Onny Valley. The full length of The Long Mynd is visible as well as the rocky top of the Stiperstones. In the next field keep the same direction, aiming for the largest tree visible directly ahead, Narrowdale Wood to the right. Cross the stile and again do the same, to eventually reach a stile just to the right of the tree you have been aiming for (actually seen as two trees close together as you approach them).

4. Once over the stile into a pasture field go slightly right to another stile and then continue ahead to a further stile. Here the view ahead is along the valley of the upper Camlad to the Welsh hills in the far distance. Again continue across a field to pass between two pine trees and then enter woodland, Oakeley Wood. Follow the wide track through Oakeley Wood and, as the track emerges to open land, the view ahead is over Bishop's Castle with Heath Mynd and Corndon Hill being prominent to its right. Proceed to the bottom of the field to pass through a gap in the hedge and go on to a lane in front of the house now visible ahead, where you turn left.

5. Follow the lane, passing the timber-framed Oakeley House (left), and reach a junction by the B4385. Do not go to the main road but turn left onto a narrower lane (Stank Lane, see map) and follow it as it climbs gently uphill. Follow the lane for almost ½ mile then, as it enters a wooded section, look for a gate at the top of the bank on the right. (If the gate is missed do not worry, just proceed to the next farm drive on the right and turn up that.) Once through the gate turn left, follow the left field edge and on reaching the farm drive turn right. Continue up the farm drive with further fine views, right and rear, over Blakeridge Wood, Bishop's Castle and then towards Heath Mynd and Corndon Hill. Just prior to the farm turn left onto a track then go through a gate to a field.

6. Follow the left field edge to cross a stile to an open field. Continue directly across (aim for the right end of the wood ahead) and then enter a short section of enclosed track. Now follow the right field edge through two fields to pass through another gate and follow the left field edge. At the next field corner cross a stile to join a very old sunken lane, which is followed back into Lydbury North. On reaching houses continue ahead to a road junction and turn right to the B4385. Here turn right to return to the Powis Arms.

WENTNOR
THE CROWN INN

This walk takes you to a section of the Secret Hills of South Shropshire that is worth finding and exploring. The route passes to the east of the village of Wentnor and along the lower western slope of The Long Mynd, giving sweeping views across, up and down, the valley of the River East Onny.

Nestling in a valley between the Shropshire landmarks of The Long Mynd and the Stiperstones lies the village of Wentnor, set on a plateau between the River East Onny and the Criftin Brook. The village, as the sturdy, solid stone dwellings attest, goes back many centuries and the small church of St Michael, although mainly 19th century, has earlier Norman sections incorporated into it. One such solidly built dwelling, the oldest parts believed to date from the 16th century, is the Crown Inn, now tastefully extended, modernised (but retaining many older features) and offering accommodation as well as food and drink. Its first use as an inn is now lost in the midst of time, but anyone entering the cosy bar with its beams and inglenook fireplace, or using the side lounge area with settee and armchairs, will immediately feel at home. Further back there is also a non-smoking dining area and a separate dining room, a spaciousness not apparent when entering the building from the front.

Once inside there is an array of good beers to tempt the palate, Worthington Bitter, Hobsons Best Bitter, Shropshire Gold and Old Speckled Hen. For lager drinkers the choice is Carling or Grolsch and for cider drinkers, Blackthorn. For wine drinkers there is an interesting selection from around the world at prices to suit a wide range of tastes. The meals available reflect the fact that the Crown Inn has an established restaurant. Bar food includes chicken curry and Shropshire sausages – delicious – served with side dishes of salad, fries or garlic bread. The main menu has such delicacies as Banana and Stilton Pot, Shrewsbury Lamb and Somerset Pork and there is a good vegetarian selection, with Hot Brie (layers of Brie, onions and apricots) being one example. All the meals are freshly prepared on the premises. Food times are 12 noon to 2 pm and 7 pm to 9 pm, all week.

Telephone: 01588 650613.

- **HOW TO GET THERE:** Wentnor is located 2 miles north of the A489 and is signposted from the hamlet of Eaton on that road. It can also be accessed by driving over The Long Mynd from Church Stretton, but that route is not for the squeamish.
- **PARKING:** At the rear of the inn via a side access (patrons only). Please advise the owners if leaving your car while you walk.
- **LENGTH OF THE WALK:** 4 miles. Map: OS Explorer 217 The Long Mynd & Wenlock Edge (GR 384928).

THE WALK

Note: Two small sections of this walk can be muddy after wet weather so suitable footwear is advised. An alternative but shorter route is shown to avoid these points but it does miss out the best views.

1. On leaving the front of the inn turn left and immediately left again. Follow the lane that becomes grassy, sweeping right, with a splendid view of the western slopes of The Long Mynd. Continue along the track to a road then, after a further 150 yards, cross a stile on the left. Follow the right fence to a gate, go through and turn left, continuing in

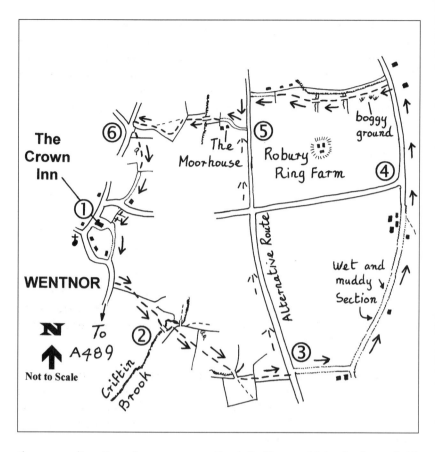

the same direction, fence now on the left. Keep within the large field, generally following the left fence, to a bridge over the Criftin Brook.

2. Cross the brook, turn left, cross a stile on the right, then go over the open field aiming to the right of the trees ahead (ignore the footbridge and stile over to the left). Cross a stile in the far hedge then go part right, across a large open field, to reach a well-built bridge in the far corner. Once over go part left to a gate in the hedge, ignoring the possibly more prominent path directly across the field. Once through the gate proceed to the top right field corner, turn left at the road and after only 25 yards turn right up a tarmac lane. (This next section, to point 5, is where you may encounter the mud. If you wish to avoid this just continue on the wider road, go over a crossroads, and proceed to point 5).

3. For the full walk go up the narrow lane turning left at the top to follow an old green lane. The view left, foliage permitting, is across the valley of the River East Onny, the rocky outcrops visible ahead/left being the Stiperstones. Directly left the view is towards Bishop's Castle and then Wales. Follow the track, negotiating any mud, to eventually pass farm buildings, left, join a tarmac lane, then reach a road and keep straight ahead.

4. Continue on the road for almost ½ a mile, admiring the more open views, left, as previously seen from the green lane. The nearest farm down on the left is located within an earthwork known as the Robury Ring. After passing Laburnum Cottage (right) cross a stile on the left, just prior to the next cottage. Now follow the stream on the right, negotiating with care the muddy patches. This section of path, down to the next road, is part of a 'short cut' on the Shropshire Way. Keep following the right fence (and for most of the way a stream), crossing stiles and plank bridges to reach a gate to a road. Here turn left then, after about 200 yards, turn right up the drive to The Moorhouse. (The area here is called Wentnor Prolly Moor, a previously wet area drained for farming in the 1800s.)

5. Follow the track as it passes to the right of the farm and enters a field to follow the left hedge. Go through another gate, with a culvert bridge over the Criftin Brook, follow the right hedge and then cross the next field to the very far left corner. At the top corner enter a lane and turn left.

6. Almost immediately turn left through a gate and then right over a stile. Now go part left and across an open field aiming for a tree near the centre. Pass to the left of the tree, join a fence and proceed to a gate in the corner. Now follow an enclosed track to another lane and cross going slightly to the left to a stile into a field. Here the right hedge is followed, over more stiles, to emerge at the car park of the Crown Inn.

MINSTERLEY
THE CROWN & SCEPTRE
❧❀❧

This attractive walk visits Poles Coppice Nature Reserve which has numerous paths and old quarries to explore.. There are also sweeping views over the Severn Valley and the Rea Valley towards Long Mountain.

The area around Minsterley has been inhabited since the earliest times, as the various hill forts attest. There was also mining, quarrying and coppicing from the 18th to the mid 19th century, a legacy of this activity being the Poles Coppice Nature Reserve, administered by Shropshire County Council and now transformed into a varied woodland habitat with walks. An ideal pub from which to visit the reserve is the Crown & Sceptre at Minsterley, now renovated and part of the Pubmaster chain. Originally more than one property, the oldest believed to be 17th century and much older than the adjacent Congregational church, today its spacious lounge bar retains the old beams; there is also a secluded dining area and a sheltered patio garden.

The range of food and drink available is enough to satisfy any hungry and thirsty rambler. The beers include Marston's Pedigree, Worthington Smooth Flow and M&B Mild. The lagers are Carling and Stella Artois, the ciders Strongbow and Red C and there is Guinness; house wines are on offer too. The food choice is from bar snacks such as toasted sandwiches and jacket potatoes through to more substantial fare including rump steak, mixed grill, chicken, fish and vegetarian dishes, as well as a range of starters and desserts and a daily specials board. Food is served all week from 12 noon to 2.30 pm and 6.30 pm to 8.30 pm; the pub also stays open in the afternoon for drinks.

Telephone: 01743 791260.

- **HOW TO GET THERE:** Minsterley is on the A488 some 9 miles south-west of Shrewsbury.
- **PARKING:** At the front of the pub (customers only) – please advise staff if leaving your car while you walk.
- **LENGTH OF THE WALK:** 4½ miles. Map: OS Explorer 216 Welshpool & Montgomery (GR 375051).

THE WALK

Note: This walk is mainly on rights of way to, and around, the nature reserve. There are many other permissive paths to explore and notice boards showing those paths are located at both of the nature reserve car parks.

1. From the pub entrance cross the car park to the main road then turn sharp right into Callow Lane. Follow this going gently uphill toward the now wooded slopes of Callow Hill with the remains of the ancient hill fort hidden by the trees. (Callow means 'bald' which the hill would have been years ago.) Continue around a right-hand bend and take a footpath going up on the left, then turn left at a wide track (the line of an old railway linking the lead mines at Snailbeach with Pontesbury). After about 100 yards turn right up a steep narrow path, just prior to gates to a quarry area, and go directly up the hill, ignoring a track going left. At a path junction keep right, on level ground (the left fork goes to the hill fort with the quarry beyond) and soon follow a fence on the left. Cross a stile to a field following the right field edge to a stile in the far corner and once over turn left.

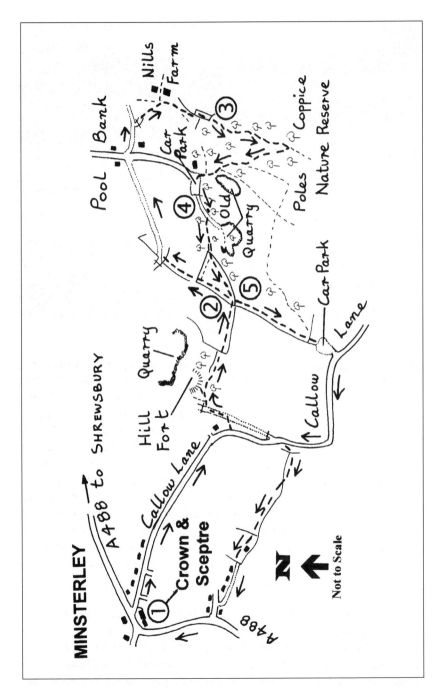

The old quarry at Poles Coppice Nature Reserve.

2. The longer walk now follows the left fence/hedge, with a sweeping view ahead across the Severn Valley into northern Shropshire. Over to the left is the wooded Pontesford Hill and the bare Earl's Hill, the lines of the Iron Age hill fort discernible (a nature reserve administered by Shropshire Wildlife Trust). Continue gently downhill to eventually join a stony track (stile and gate). Turn right and follow the track to a road at Pool Bank. Cross the road, continue ahead on another stony track, a bridleway, for 200 yards then leave it, joining a grassy track ahead via a bridlegate. Continue ahead to approach Nills Farm (Earl's Hill beyond) then sweep right keeping the farm buildings on your left (ignore the bridleway through the farm). Immediately past the farm take the path going down to the left to join the fence line (turn off by a large tree). At the far corner cross a stile, turn right on an enclosed path, enter a woodland and continue straight ahead.

3. Follow this meandering path through woodland for about 500 yards to meet a bridleway coming from the opposite direction, here turn sharp right and follow the bridleway going uphill – watch for evidence of horses hooves to indicate that you have joined the bridleway. At the next path junction go right (the left path goes to Callow Lane) and again go right at a second track junction. (At this second junction the path to the left also goes to Callow Lane passing old quarry workings, yet more paths to explore if time permits.) Continue along the bridleway (ignore a footpath to the right) to reach the Polesgate Car Park and turn left.

4. From the parking area take the wide track, with the barrier, entering coppiced woodland then, after 200 yards, take a narrow track going right. Before doing this it is worth visiting the old quarry and explore a little, the area now being re-colonised by trees and plants. To continue the walk follow the narrow path which meanders downhill to cross a footbridge to a kissing gate. In the next field turn left and follow the field edge to the very top corner and use the gate or adjacent stile to the field beyond.

5. Follow the right hedge to eventually reach the Callow Lane Car Park and then turn right at the road. Here the panoramic view ahead is over the Rea Valley towards Long Mountain. Follow the road as it sweeps right then, as a gated track comes into view ahead (the old rail line crossed earlier) look for a narrow path on the left that goes downhill and back in the direction just travelled (if this is missed the road continues back to Minsterley). At the bottom enter a field, follow the right hedge, cross a stile and continue as before but with the hedge now on the left. Proceed through a playing field (ignore stiles on the left). Go along a drive and at an estate road turn left. Continue to the A488 then turn right and follow it back to the Crown & Sceptre.

WALK 17

MYDDLE
THE RED LION

A delightful walk through the rich pastoral North Shropshire countryside using a section of the Marches Way, visiting Merrington Green Nature Reserve, then returning via quiet country lanes, over fields and through woods, with a superb view towards the Shropshire hills.

The village of Myddle has a history going back to Saxon times, was the site of a Norman castle (once the abode of Humphrey Kynaston, the highwayman of Nesscliffe) and has an interesting old inn, the Red Lion. The main part of the inn (the bar and restaurant areas) was once a barn, thought to have been located adjacent to the church but subsequently dismantled, moved to its present location, then used as a dwelling and an ale house, all this prior to 1701. A framed drawing of the structural details of the building, with historical notes, is on the wall in the bar and is well worth reading. Today this fine old inn has a wealth of old beams, a roomy, comfortable bar with a large fireplace, a separate restaurant area and, in the more recent part of the building, a games room. The external features are also worth viewing, particularly the leaded windows and the ornate chimneys.

As interesting as the pub itself is the range of beers and lagers available. The main beers are Marston's Pedigree, Banks's Bitter and Guinness. The lagers are Kronenbourg 1664, Harp and Foster's, and for cider drinkers there is a choice of Strongbow or Woodpecker. Also available is a selection of house wine. At lunchtimes the food choice is from the bar meals menu which encompasses sandwiches, cold meat salads, ploughman's lunches, soup and a selection of hot dishes (their speciality is steak and kidney pie), and the evening menu includes a range of steaks, grills and fish. Both menus vary according to the season of the year and the local produce obtainable, all meals being freshly prepared. Food is usually available each lunchtime and evening, (except Monday evening) from 12 noon to 2 pm and 7 pm to 8.30 pm – these times can be flexible so it may be worth telephoning beforehand if food is required for larger groups of walkers.

Telephone: 01939 290951.

- **HOW TO GET THERE:** Myddle is just off the A528 Shrewsbury to Ellesmere road, some 7 miles north of Shrewsbury. The inn is near the centre of the village.
- **PARKING:** Parking is available for customers at the front and side/rear of the inn. If leaving your car while you walk please use the side/rear car park and advise the owners.
- **LENGTH OF THE WALK:** 5½ miles. Map: OS Explorer 241 Shrewsbury (GR 468239).

THE WALK

1. From the Red Lion go to the road, turn right and follow it past the school and The Glebelands (a name indicating that the land was once owned by the church). Continue past the church, St Peter's, which has sections dating from the 17th (tower), 18th (nave) and 19th centuries. The site of the castle, now occupied by farm buildings, is located behind the church. Continue along the road to a point about 50 yards beyond the last house on the left and turn left through a gate. Now turn right and follow the right hedge as it meanders around (the hills visible in the far distance include The Long Mynd and the Breiddens) to join a track via another gate. Once through turn left to follow a dirt track, a

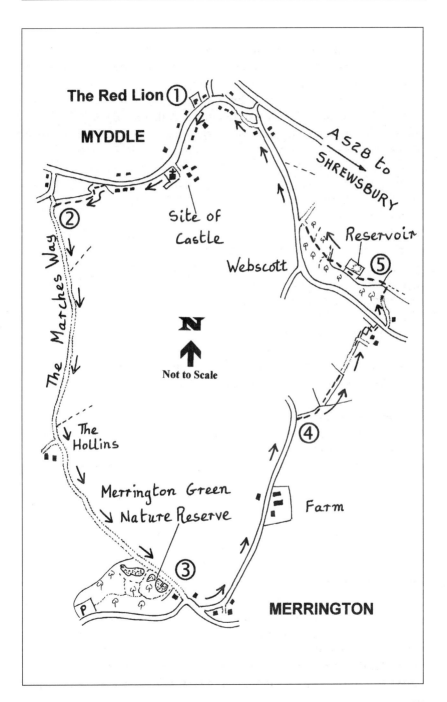

Merrington Green Nature Reserve.

bridleway. (This path along the field edge is a permissive path provided as a result of removing a hedge – it differs from the route as shown on the OS map.)

2. Now follow the wide bridleway, ignoring the stile at a bend in the path. The route from here to Merrington is part of the Marches Way, a long distance trail which runs through the Welsh Marches counties from Chester to Cardiff, providing a 204 mile alternative route to the Offa's Dyke Path. Continue along the wide bridleway for almost 2 miles, the surface varying from grass to dirt to stones. On approaching a path junction by The Hollins keep ahead/left and eventually reach the Merrington Green Nature Reserve. The first access point reached, from this bridleway, is a plank causeway going into the trees on the right. Another access point, with a pond, viewing platform and handy seat for a coffee break, is about 200 yards further on. As this is the halfway point of the walk it is an ideal place to stop and explore.

3. The nature reserve is administered by the Shropshire Wildlife Trust and consists of 12 hectares of medieval common land with several ponds. On leaving the reserve rejoin the bridleway and continue in the same direction as before. At the road continue ahead for about 150 yards and turn left up a lane (to Webscott and Myddle), noticing the old water pump at the corner. A wall plaque records appreciation to the Slaney family for providing a well for the hamlet of Merrington. The route is now along this country lane with the wide verges providing an excellent habitat for butterflies. Continue to a point some 500 yards past farm buildings to reach a stile in the hedge on the right, located just beyond a passing place but prior to a left-hand bend in the road.

4. Once over follow the left hedge for just over 100 yards to cross a fence on the left. The line of the right of way, from here to the next road, was officially diverted in late 1996; this book uses the new path but some old OS maps will still show the previous route. Now follow the right hedge/fence (old hedge with oak trees and bushes) then join a track across an open section of field. As the track turns right keep straight ahead, over a sleeper bridge, to follow the right hedge to the far right corner of the field. Here cross the stile and follow the left hedge/fence around to reach a road and then turn right. Go along the road for only 40 yards and turn left up a concrete drive. Follow the drive past a house continuing on a dirt track that sweeps right, going uphill to reach an open field. Here turn left and go through a gate into another field.

5. The route is now directly across the field aiming to the left of the mound ahead, a reservoir. Here a dramatic vista opens left, over North Shropshire towards the Shropshire hills and Wales. The range of hills visible, right to left, are the Breiddens, Long Mountain (both in Wales), the Stiperstones, The Long Mynd, Caer Caradoc, The Lawley and Brown Clee Hill. On reaching the reservoir cross the stile and follow the path enclosed by a wall and the reservoir fence. (This path may be overgrown and, whilst it is possible to use the field around the other side of the reservoir, that is not a right of way.) From the stile at the far side of the reservoir follow the left fence for almost 100 yards and cross a stile on the left to enter the wood (caution, deep quarry to the left). Follow the main path downhill and at a fork keep right, continuing downhill through the wood, entering a wide gully. On reaching the road turn right to follow this pleasant country lane back to Myddle. After reaching the houses look for a bridleway on the left, just past Silverbriars, follow this to rejoin the road and continue ahead back to the Red Lion.

LLYNCLYS, NEAR OSWESTRY
THE WHITE LION

A varied and interesting walk that takes you over Crickheath Hill and visits a section of Offa's Dyke, along the top of Blodwel Rock, then continuing over the Llynclys Common Nature Reserve with its numerous paths for exploration. There are also wonderful views over northern Shropshire and to The Wrekin, the Breiddens, Long Mountain and also across the Tanat Valley into Wales.

The White Lion is situated on an important crossroads, the A483 running north from Welshpool to Oswestry and Wrexham, and the A495 which links with the B4396 (Knockin and Shrewsbury road) at Llynclys. Thus the location was ideal for a coaching inn as the White Lion (at one time called the George) was when built in the late 18th century. By the start of the 20th century it had become the White Lion Inn, a white lion being the symbol of English monarchs, the red lion that of the Welsh princes. Over the years the premises have been considerably extended and the entrance position changed so today there is a large sub-divided bar area (the oldest part of the building) and a dining section that was once the alighting place for the coaches. Upstairs there is a games room and children's area and outside there is a beer garden and a space for touring caravans.

Now that the coaching days have gone and quarrying has ceased in the region, this pub now relies on passing trade and the food and drink available reflect this. Lunchtime bar snacks include filled rolls, full breakfast, fish and chips and beef hotpot. There are daily specials too, such as my roast duck (very tasty). The evening menu (also available at lunchtime if required) has more substantial meals such as sirloin or fillet steak, garlic chicken and gammon steak as well as starters and puddings, Vegetarians are also well catered for. For liquid refreshment there is John Smith's Extra Smooth Bitter and a guest beer such as Courage Directors. There are also Heineken and Stella Artois lagers, Strongbow cider, Guinness and house wines. Food is available from 12 noon to 2.45 pm on Mondays, Thursdays and Fridays and from 6 pm to 10 pm on Monday to Friday evenings; also all day, 12 noon onwards, on Saturday (to 10 pm) and Sunday (to 9 pm).

Telephone: 01691 830357.

- **HOW TO GET THERE:** The White Lion will be found some 4 miles south of Oswestry at the junction of the A483 and the A495.
- **PARKING:** There is a car park at the side of the pub for customers; please advise staff if leaving your car while you walk.
- **LENGTH OF THE WALK:** 4 miles. Map: OS Explorer 240 Oswestry (GR 282241).

THE WALK

Note: The whole area of the Llanymynech, Crickheath and Llynclys Hills has been mined and quarried since Roman times and there is a maze of tracks, bridleways and footpaths. This walk is an introduction to the latter two hills and there is a leaflet, usually available from the local Tourist Information Centres, that shows all of the paths over Llynclys Common.

1. From the White Lion cross the A495, follow the A483 towards Pant then, after only 100 yards, take a track going off to the right. After a further 100 yards leave the track to enter a field (on the right) and follow the left field edge, with Llynclys Hill up on the right. Continue

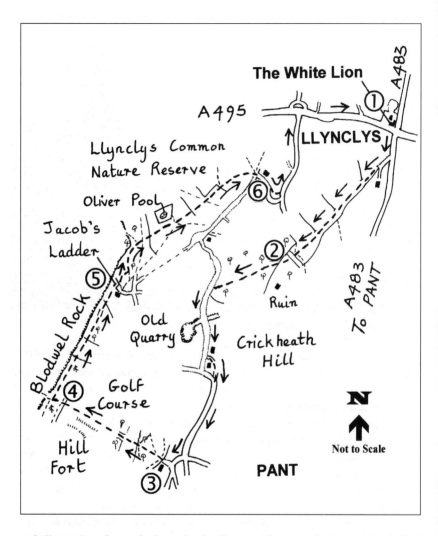

uphill passing through three hedge lines with a good view to the left of the Shropshire Plain and The Wrekin. After passing through the third hedge go part right to a stile in the tree line ahead (not the stile in the top left corner). Pass through a band of trees then go part right to a stile in the tree line now ahead/right.

2. Initially follow a path enclosed by shrubs and trees then go directly across more open land to the hedge at the very far side (the hills visible to the left are Breidden Hill, with Admiral Rodney's Pillar on top and

View across the Tanat Valley into Wales from Blodwel Rock.

Long Mountain to the right). Cross a stile (about 40 yards to the right of a gate in the far left corner) and turn left along a track, then watch for a deep cutting on the right. The now 'filled in' ravine was once crossed by a bridge (Black Bridge), beneath which a tramway from a quarry on the right ran down to the Ellesmere Canal in the valley. Continue to a dwelling on the left then, just past the garden, cross a stile on the left. Take the enclosed track to a lane, turn left and follow the lane, past houses, to a junction of four roads. Turn right and after 100 yards turn right again, up a drive, to a kissing gate at the side of the house.

3. Take the path going directly up the hill then, after only 20 yards, take the left fork. Follow the enclosed path uphill and proceed directly across the fairway of a golf course. Join another enclosed track to reach a further section of the golf course, again proceeding directly ahead and soon following a shallow ditch on the left. Up to the left the outline of parts of an ancient hill fort are evident. Again enter trees and soon cross a stile into denser coniferous woodland, proceeding directly uphill to an isolated stile on the ridge. Do not cross the stile but turn right to go onto, and then follow, the ridge of Blodwel Rock.

4. This ridge route, trees to the right, very steep drop to the left, is on the line of Offa's Dyke but it does not form part of the official path as the workings of Llynclys Quarry (visible later) obliterated part of the Dyke. Follow the ridge with numerous points to appreciate the view across the Tanat Valley into Wales, crossing several stiles and a footbridge (over a deep ravine with a steep drop to the left). Eventually go downhill to reach some wooden steps, known locally as Jacob's Ladder.

5. The next section is through the Llynclys Common Nature Reserve which is administered by the Shropshire Wildlife Trust. There are numerous rights of way and permissive paths over this reserve; the route of this walk uses both types but avoids the bridleways as they can be muddy.

After descending the steps cross a stile, turn left and in less than 10 yards turn right to enter trees (the path may be obscured by bracken in summer). Exit the trees and continue ahead, trees to the left – this area is covered in knapweed in summer and is a haven for butterflies. Reach a path junction and turn left onto a more prominent path which goes downhill, steep slope to the left. At the next path junction go ahead to a gate, continue in the same direction to join a fence, then on reaching an open space turn left. (The fenced area on the left is around Oliver Pool, now a thriving wildlife pond, which was re-excavated in 1990 and is accessible.) Proceed to a large gate and continue ahead on a wide track, ignoring paths to left and right. Soon join a wire fence on the left and go through another bridlegate, again keeping ahead to eventually emerge at a path junction. Here go straight ahead to join a wide stony track.

6. Follow the track, passing a house on the left (Beulah Lodge), then as the track sweeps right look for a narrow path going into the trees on the left, just past an electricity pole. (If the narrow path is missed the wide track sweeps around to the same point.) Follow this path steeply downhill to a lane and continue along that to reach the A495. Here turn right and follow the road back to the White Lion.

CANDY, NEAR OSWESTRY
THE OLD MILL INN

Here is a wealth of history from a short, enjoyable walk. The route proceeds from the valley of the River Morda to the deserted Oswestry Racecourse and returns on the Offa's Dyke Path with sweeping views across North Shropshire and glimpses towards Wales.

In a steep-sided valley of the River Morda (named Candy on some OS maps) stands the Old Mill Inn, with the Offa's Dyke Path passing the front entrance. Originally named the Llanforda Mill, corn production ceased in the early 1900s when the unfortunate owner was crushed to death in the moving cog wheels. In the mid 1970s it was partially damaged by fire and then restored as a restaurant and pub in the early 1980s. Today it attracts customers from all over the country, and from abroad, as it offers accommodation for people walking Offa's Dyke. The solidly-built inn now has a large lounge/bar, a games room, a non-smoking dining/conservatory and extensive gardens with a children's play area. A great base from which to do this walk and explore the local countryside.

Known locally for its good food the menu choice varies according to the season but will always include dishes from around the world. Examples are grills (superb fillet steak), Honey and Herb Roast Turkey, Texas Style Ribs, Malaysian and Indian curries and many others, everything from a wholesome bar snack to a full meal. The beers are Friary Meux Best Bitter, Tetley Bitter, Old Speckled Hen, Guinness and guests. Cider drinkers have Woodpecker and Strongbow, the lager is Carlsberg and there is a comprehensive wine list. The inn is open all week except Monday and Tuesday, food being available from 12 noon to 2.30 pm and 7 pm to 9.30 pm.

Telephone: 01691 657058.

- **HOW TO GET THERE:** The use of a map is advised. Take the Trefonen road out of Oswestry and once past the Ashfield Hotel take the next turn right, signposted to Llansilin. Then take the next lane right, narrow and steep, down to the inn.
- **PARKING:** There is a large parking area opposite the hotel but please advise the hotel before leaving your car whilst you walk.
- **LENGTH OF THE WALK:** 4 miles. Map: OS Explorer 240 Oswestry (GR 256282).

THE WALK

1. From the front of the inn cross the car park and the River Morda then turn right along the lane. Continue uphill passing Walnut Tree Cottage, on the right, then as the lane levels turn left through a large gate. Immediately turn right and go up through the trees to a stile – the path may be indistinct but it is a right of way. Go straight up the field to another stile then go part left to cross open parkland, the view sweeps from The Wrekin around to the Breiddens and Long Mountain. On encountering a grassy track turn right then keep straight ahead following the flattened grass towards a large gate and stile; do not cross but turn left to follow the right fence line. (The old walls visible beyond the gate are the ruins of the walled garden of Llanforda Hall.)

2. Continue to follow the right fence line as it turns left to go up to the top right field corner. Cross the stile, turn right, then follow the right field edge as it turns left. At the top corner cross a farm drive then go slightly right, over a field, to enter woodland. The path now meanders,

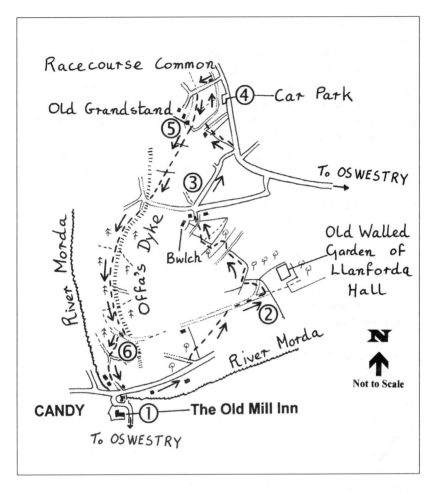

generally to the left, to eventually leave the wood via a ditch crossing and stile on the right. Follow the right fence for some 100 yards to cross a stile on the right, then go part left and diagonally across the field, aiming for the left end of the buildings ahead (Bwlch). Cross a farm track (stiles), go part right to a large gate then follow a drive to a road then continue along the lane opposite.

3. The lane is now followed with a wonderful view, to the right, across the northern Shropshire Plain towards Cheshire and Staffordshire. Soon join another road and almost immediately turn left over a stile to follow the left field edge to the top left corner (worth turning around to admire the view). Pass a house, left, to cross a drive and continue straight ahead (may be overgrown with bracken in the summer). After about 50 yards reach a wide track and turn right – this was part of the racetrack of the Oswestry Racecourse which operated between 1777 and 1848 – following it to reach the car park. (A participant was 'Mad Jack' Mytton, whose name is remembered by a 70 mile bridleway across South Shropshire, the Jack Mytton Way – see Walk 11.) By the car park there are seats and a Skyline Map of the view eastwards.

4. Continue following the wide track northwards to reach a gravel track and turn left. (The area of the old racecourse, known as Racecourse Common and administered by Oswestry Borough Council, extends northwards over the B4580 and can be explored at leisure.) Follow the gravel track to the next junction and turn sharp left onto a grassy track – there are two parallel tracks, the one on the right is the old racetrack. Pass the ruins of the old grandstand with a viewpoint and more Skyline Maps (the view now obscured by trees), continue to a sculpture of horses' heads and a saddle, then take the path forking right. The Offa's Dyke Path is now followed back to the start, so watch for the acorn symbol.

5. The path now enters woodland, the Dyke being over to the right but not yet visible. Continue through a mixture of woodland and open path to a track junction; here turn right, passing through the line of the Dyke, then immediately sharp left, now following the base of Offa's Dyke. It is now possible to appreciate how prominent the Dyke would have been when viewed from the west and not obscured by the modern tree plantation, which unfortunately also hides the view to the west. The route now follows the base of the Dyke for well over ½ mile, ignoring paths to right and left to meet a wide track at a T junction.

6. Here turn right then, after 20 yards, turn left to go steeply downhill (the path leaving the line of the Dyke). On joining another track turn left and immediately take the right fork. This path is then followed down to a house drive which in turn is followed to a lane with the Old Mill Inn opposite.

LOPPINGTON, NEAR ELLESMERE
THE DICKIN ARMS

A really enjoyable and gentle stroll, mainly across pasture land, from the attractive village of Loppington, through the hamlet of Brownheath and back over fields to the south. This is a shorter walk to contrast with the longer rambles at nearby Whixall and Myddle.

The village of Loppington (a settlement at the time of the Domesday survey) is today a mixture of old and new, with timber-framed dwellings blending with the later additions including the Dickin Arms, named after the then local landowner, Col Dickin. Built in the late 18th century the inn was fully refurbished in the mid 1990s and today, as the only pub in the village (the other pub, the Blacksmith's Arms, is now a private house), it caters for both locals and residents with its excellent range of food and drink. Customers have a choice of using the combined bar and games room, the attractive lounge bar, ideal for lunchtime meals and a quiet drink, or the non-smoking dining room that comes into its own for evening meals. As might be expected from an older building both bars have a wealth of exposed beams. Another link with the past is outside the front door, the only existing bull-baiting ring left in Shropshire, reputed to have been last used in 1835.

To fortify the intrepid rambler the pub offers a comprehensive range of food, from baguettes through to a full breakfast, home-made Steak and Ale Pie, fish, chicken, pasta or omelettes (my own choice, mushroom omelette, being very good), as well as a specials board. Evening diners can choose from such dishes as Peppered Fillet Steak, Duo of Cod and Salmon and Shropshire Lamb Steak. To quench the thirst the standard beers are Draught Bass and Caffrey's as well as a guest beer such as Bateman XXXB. In addition there is Worthington Creamflow, Guinness and also Strongbow cider. The lager choice is Grolsch or Carling and there is a list of wines from around the world. Food is available all week, except Monday, from 12 noon to 2.30 pm and 7 pm to 9.30 pm.

Telephone: 01939 233471.

- **HOW TO GET THERE:** The pub is at the centre of Loppington on the B4397. The village is signposted from both the A528 and the B5063.
- **PARKING:** There is a pub car park available for use by patrons. Please advise the owner if leaving your car while you walk.
- **LENGTH OF THE WALK:** 3 miles. Map: OS Explorer 241 Shrewsbury (GR 471293).

THE WALK

1. From the front door of the pub turn left and pass the bull-baiting ring set in the tarmac road, between the pub and the war memorial. Cross the B4397, turn right and after only 30 yards turn left onto an enclosed track. At the track end enter a field, follow the left field edge to a stile then cross the next field to the very far right corner. Now follow the right hedge to a stile about 30 yards after turning a corner and again follow the right hedge. Pass a pond on the left (a peaceful place to ponder!) and cross a stile to a road. Take the narrow lane opposite and after only 60 yards cross a stile on the left. Now turn part right to cross an arable field to a stile in the far hedge, probably hidden until reached, a good aiming point is the tall tree well to the left of the cottage visible ahead. (The right of way is directly across the field but, if this route is blocked by crops, it is possible to walk around the left side of the field.) On reaching the road turn right.

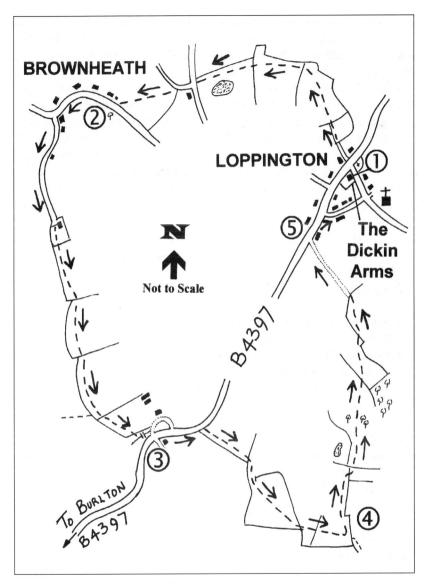

2. Now follow the road through the scattered hamlet of Brownheath and take the next turning left, by some farm buildings. Follow this narrow lane to the far end to then pass through a house garden to a stile in the far fence. (The route may be signposted by the owners; also please respect their privacy as this is their garden.) In the next field follow the line of the right hedge to a gate near the far right corner. Keep the same direction over the next field to another gate and then again follow the right hedge, crossing another stile. On approaching a house drive use the stile on the right, then turn left and after 15 yards turn right to cross a bridge over a brook. At the B4397 turn left.

3. Follow the road for about 300 yards around bends then, after the second bend (sweeping left), take the second gate on the right (a stile, possibly overgrown, to its right). Follow the right fence to a stile in the far right corner and then turn right to pass through a gap in the hedge. Now go part left and diagonally across the field to the very far left corner. Cross a stile and then a narrow field and proceed directly across the next field to the far hedge; on reaching the hedge turn left (if you do find a well-hidden stile beyond the hedge do not cross).

4. Follow the right hedge and, just prior to reaching the very far right corner cross a stile on the right. Now turn left and then go over another stile, initially following the left hedge and then over the field, passing to the left of two trees, to cross a stile in the far hedge. Once over go part left, aiming for the church tower, and eventually reach another stile (initially hidden from view) just beyond a kink in the hedge. Once over turn left, cutting across the field edge, to another stile in the next corner. Cross this and follow an old green lane to again reach the B4397 and turn right.

5. Follow the road (the large house on the right as you leave the green lane was once a pub) and soon sweep right into Scholars Lane. Follow this (notice the old barn) to reach the next road junction with the parish church opposite. St Michael's church is of mainly 14th century construction but had to be extensively repaired after the Civil War, having been involved in a skirmish between Parliamentary and Royalist troops. The churchyard with its array of old headstones is worth visiting. On leaving the churchyard turn right to return to the Dickin Arms.